Reading Contemporary Britain:

15 Critical Views of Culture and Society

Christopher J. Armstrong／Anthony Piccolo／板倉厳一郎 著

松柏社

はじめに

　イギリスというと、何を思い浮かべるだろう？　ハリー・ポッター、シャーロック・ホームズ、アリス、サッカー、アフタヌーン・ティー……。

　だが、この伝統の国は新たな局面を迎えつつある。B級グルメの定番フィッシュ・アンド・チップスはチキン・ティッカ・マサラに王座を奪われ、さらに最近では中華の野菜炒めが一番人気となった。いまや旧植民地のインド出身者だけでなく、50万人以上のポーランド系住民を抱えている。2011年の国勢調査ではキリスト教信者が13％も減り、無宗教が10％も伸びた。2014年にスコットランド独立をめぐる住民投票が行われたことは記憶に新しい。この国の伝統だけでなく、今を知ることもまた大切なのだ。

　本書は、現代のイギリスの諸相を批評的に見直すものである。収録された15のエッセイは、トピックも宗教、人種、ジェンダー、戦争、スポーツ、教育、監視社会と多岐にわたり、変化を続ける21世紀のイギリス社会に深くメスを入れている。イギリス文化や社会に対し、時として批判的な視点も取り入れながら、イギリス映画、ドキュメンタリー映画、テレビ番組、ニュース、書籍や雑誌・新聞記事、最近の研究書や社会評論なども取り入れている。

　本書は基本的に大学の語学教材であるが、イギリス文化研究やイギリス社会研究のような講義やゼミでも使用できる。読解問題が最新のTOEFL® Test形式に対応しているので、テスト対策にも適している。

▼本書のアクティビティは以下のように構成されている。

1. Brainstorming on the Topicでは、トピックについて知っていることをどんどん挙げていくことで他の学生と知識を共有する
2. Comprehensionでは、600語程度のエッセイを読み、TOEFL® iBTのフォーマットの問題を解くことで読解力を高める
3. Summaryでは、ある段落の正しい要約文を選ぶことでエッセイの内容をもう一度振り返る
4. Discussionには一般的な問題とやや専門的な問題がついているので、エッセイの主張を自分なりに評価したり、同じ題材について自分の意見を述べたりすることで英語力のみならず考える力も養える
5. Homework/Researchでは、関連する映画などを視聴することで取り上げられた題材についての理解をより深いものにできる

　なお、本書の作成には松柏社の森有紀子氏ならびに永野啓子氏にお世話になった。森氏の呼びかけがあってこそ本書は生まれたのだし、編集作業での永野氏の的確な助言や指摘がなければ本書は形にならなかった。ここに謝意を表したい。

2014年9月　筆者一同

■ 凡例

本書で用いられている略称は以下の通り。

名→名詞　形→形容詞　自動→自動詞　副→副詞　他動→他動詞　対→対義語

■ 問題文のパターンについて

TOEFL® TestのReadingの問題にはパターンがあるので、覚えておくとよい。

▶[i] 同意語を聞く問題◀

The word/phrase ... in paragraph X is closest in meaning to
（X段落にある...という単語／熟語は次のどれと意味が一番近いか）

▶[ii] 著者の意図を問う問題◀

・The author refers to ... to show that
（著者は何を証明するために...に触れているのか）

・The author cites ... as an example of
（著者は何の例として...を挙げているのか）

▶[iii] 文章を挿入する問題◀

[A], [B], [C] and [D] indicate where the following sentence can be added to paragraph X.
（以下の英文は段落Xの[A]〜[D]のどこに入れるのが適当か）

CONTENTS

はじめに ……………………………………………………………………… ii

Chapter 1 **The Lion, the Wizards and the Dust:** ……… 1
Children's Literature and Religion

Chapter 2 **Gender in the UK:** LGBT Issues ……………… 7

Chapter 3 **Queen's English, Prince's English** ……………… 13

Chapter 4 **Class and the British Way of Life** ……………… 19

Chapter 5 **Football and Language** ………………………… 25

Chapter 6 **Education in Britain** …………………………… 31

Chapter 7 **World War I:** One Hundred Years After ……… 37

Chapter 8 **Mod and Modern Britain** ……………………… 43

Chapter 9 **"A green and pleasant land"?:** ………………… 49
Social Order and the English Countryside

Chapter 10 **Monty Python's *Life of Brian*:** ………………… 55
Comedy or Blasphemy?

Chapter 11 ***Sherlock*:** A Holmes for Our Time ……………… 61

Chapter 12 **"Century of Strangers":** ………………………… 67
Immigrants from Former British Colonies

Chapter 13 **The UK:** A Surveillance Society ………………… 73

Chapter 14 **Refugees and Asylum Seekers in the UK** …… 79

Chapter 15 **Not Always What It Seems:** …………………… 85
England in Irish Films

人名・映画作品名・企業名など ……………………………………… 91

Chapter 1

The Lion, the Wizards and the Dust:
Children's Literature and Religion

映画『ハリー・ポッターと秘密の部屋』(2002)より

Warming-Up Activities:

1. Brainstorming on the Topic

『不思議の国のアリス』、『ナルニア国ものがたり』、『ハリー・ポッター』など、イギリスは多くの児童文学の傑作を生み出してきた。児童文学はどのように宗教と関わっているのだろう？ イギリスの児童文学および宗教について知っている人物やキーワードを英語で書き出してみよう。

2. Vocabulary

☐ religion	名 宗教(形 religious)	☐ intend	他動 〜を意図する
☐ ban	名 禁止 他動 〜を禁止する	☐ associate	他動 〜を(with …に)結びつける
☐ acquire	他動 〜を獲得する	☐ expel	他動 〜を追い出す、〜を退学にする
☐ interpretation	名 解釈(他動 interpret)	☐ indicate	他動 〜を示す
☐ campaign	自動 運動を起こす	☐ decline	名 衰退、没落

Reading

Do you know the Harry Potter books (1997-2007) were banned from many public school libraries in the United States? And why they were banned? Because at Hogwarts School of Witchcraft and Wizardry, students learn and eventually acquire a full command of magic. According to a rigid interpretation of the Bible, God only can exercise supernatural powers. Those who use supernatural powers—such as Moses and Jesus Christ—are the chosen ones who do it to provide evidence of God's existence and powers. Magic should not be taught at school. Nor should it be used for personal, secular purposes. Therefore, the Harry Potter series is supposed to be anti-Christian. In no other country was the ban enforced more extensively than in the United States, but many people expressed similar concerns about the series in the UK and in Europe. However, this "anti-Potter" movement did not last long. After all, many people interpret the Bible more flexibly. Even in the US, parents and children had campaigned against the ban until it was finally lifted.

This anecdote points to the special position of children's literature in the West. Children's literature has almost always been adults' expression of their ideas of what a child should be. At first, it was used for children's education. In 17th-century France, Charles Perrault published a collection of fairytales (1697), arguably the first book of children's literature. As the book was intended for Parisian upper-class circles, he added "*Moralités*" and "*Autre moralités*", verses containing Christian teaching, at the end of each. Throughout the 18th century, Perrault's tales inspired English authors to produce equally didactic, Christian tales. This trend had lasted until the mid-19th century, the "Golden Age" of British children's literature. Many writers started to rewrite childhood as a site of salvation. [A] In *The Secret Garden* (1911), for example, children lead an adult into the garden, which signals his imaginary return to the Garden of Eden. [B] Whether writers wanted to indoctrinate children in Christianity or re-create them as innocent and noble beings, they had to produce something compatible with Christian teaching. [C] Therefore, even a hint of anti-Christian impulses could ignite criticism. [D]

In this respect, two famous series of 20th-century British children's literature form a striking contrast. *The Chronicles of Narnia* (1950-56) brings this Christian tradition to the pinnacle of high art, whilst *His Dark Materials* (1995-2000) shatters it to pieces. In the first Narnia book, *The Lion, the Witch and the Wardrobe* (1950), a wise lion named Aslan dies on the Stone Table for a boy's sin and rises from the dead to save the world. This episode is obviously modelled on the biblical account of Jesus' crucifixion and resurrection. In Disney's recent film version, the evil White Witch's minions bawl at Aslan in an uncivilised manner that reminds us of Roman soldiers and people mocking Jesus on his way to Calvary. By contrast, *His Dark Materials* openly attacks the Magisterium, a fictional church. In the first book, *Northern Lights* (1995), the heroine Lyra's uncle—father, in fact—Lord Asriel discovers a mysterious particle called "Dust", which the Magisterium associates with "Original Sin". "Dust" is indeed like the "Forbidden Fruit" of the Tree of Knowledge in the Bible, as it makes the eater self-conscious. Adam and Eve eat the Fruit and are expelled from the Garden of Eden, which is called the "Fall." In the third book, *The Amber Spyglass* (2000), however, Lyra and Will eat the fruit and *fall* in love. Instead of teaching children Christianity, *His Dark Materials* is meant to teach them atheism. The popularity of the series may indicate the decline of Christian faith and the rise of atheism.

映画『ナルニア国物語――ライオンと魔女』(2005)より

Notes

● l. 3：**Hogwarts School of Witchcraft and Wizardry** ホグワーツ魔法学校(『ハリー・ポッター』シリーズの舞台) ● l. 3：**eventually** 副 結局は ● l. 4：**rigid** 形 堅い、柔軟性のない ● l. 5-6：**Moses and Jesus Christ** 旧約聖書に登場する預言者モーセと新約聖書に登場する救世主イエス・キリスト ● l. 9：**enforce** 他動 ～を施行する ● l. 9：**extensively** 副 広く ● l. 14：**anecdote** 名 逸話 ● l. 17：**arguably** 副 異論のあるところではあるが、ほぼ間違いなく ● l. 19：**verse** 名 韻文(詩になっている文章) ● l. 23：**salvation** 名 救済 ● l. 26：**compatible** 形 (with ～と)矛盾しない ● l. 32：**whilst** 接 = while ● l. 34：**the Stone Table** 石の舞台 ● l. 36：**crucifixion** 名 磔刑、特にイエス・キリストの磔刑 ● l. 36：**resurrection** 名 復活 ● l. 41：**particle** 名 粒子 ● l. 42：**the Forbidden Fruit of the Tree of Knowledge** 旧約聖書で神が食べることを禁じた知恵の木の禁断の果実(リンゴの実) ● l. 46：**atheism** 名 無神論

Comprehension

1. In paragraph 1, the author suggests
   (A) the Harry Potter series hadn't been published in the US for a long time.
   (B) many characters eventually become evil wizards and witches in the Harry Potter series.
   (C) some British people considered the Harry Potter series to be anti-Christian.
   (D) those who banned the Harry Potter series interpret the Bible very flexibly.

2. Personal, secular purposes in paragraph 1 include all the following EXCEPT:
   (A) to repair your glasses
   (B) to remove a cancer from your grandfather's lung
   (C) to convert unbelieving criminals to Christianity
   (D) to end the war that is taking place in Africa

3. The word lifted in paragraph 1 is closest in meaning to
   (A) cancelled
   (B) ignored
   (C) put
   (D) strengthened

4. Which of the following is the second role of children's literature in paragraph 2?
   (A) good intentions of Parisian upper-class circles
   (B) an inspiration for 18th-century authors
   (C) adults' conversion to Christianity
   (D) the projection of adults' desire

5. The word didactic in paragraph 2 is closest in meaning to
   (A) domestic
   (B) instructive
   (C) threatening
   (D) worthwhile

6. The phrase <u>indoctrinate children in Christianity</u> in paragraph 2 is closest in meaning to
   - (A) impose children on Christianity
   - (B) impart children to Christianity
   - (C) send children to Christianity
   - (D) teach children Christianity

7. [A], [B], [C] and [D] indicate where the following sentence can be added to paragraph 2. Mark the answer on your answer sheet.
   That is what readers' parents expected from them.

8. The word <u>pinnacle</u> in paragraph 3 is closest in meaning to
   - (A) basis
   - (B) height
   - (C) identity
   - (D) meaning

9. Why does the author most likely use the phrase <u>By contrast</u> in paragraph 3?
   - (A) Because *The Chronicles of Narnia* is better as a literary series than *His Dark Materials*.
   - (B) Because *The Chronicles of Narnia* is slightly more Christian than *His Dark Materials*.
   - (C) Because *The Chronicles of Narnia* and *His Dark Materials* use different narratives from the Bible.
   - (D) Because *The Chronicles of Narnia* applauds Christianity but *His Dark Materials* attacks it.

10. The author refers to <u>"Dust"</u> in paragraph 3 in order to show
    - (A) why the Magisterium is criticised so severely in *His Dark Materials*.
    - (B) that Lord Asriel of *His Dark Materials* resemble Satan of the Bible.
    - (C) how a story from the Bible is parodied in *His Dark Materials*.
    - (D) why the story of Adam and Eve inspired the author of *His Dark Materials*.

Summary

Read the sentences below and choose the statement that best summarises paragraph 3.

(A) *The Chronicles of Narnia* and *His Dark Materials* have opposite attitudes towards Christianity.

(B) *The Chronicles of Narnia* and *His Dark Materials* have opposite views of the decline of Christianity.

(C) *The Chronicles of Narnia* and *His Dark Materials* have opposite ideas about children's growth.

Discussion

1. Do you feel the author provides an accurate account of British children's literature and religion? Draw on your knowledge of films or novels to support your view.

2. How do you compare British children's books with the film versions (Disney etc.) in their treatment of such social/cultural issues as Christian faith, religious diversity and atheism?

Homework / Research

Find out more on British children's literature. Read novels and watch films; such as *Alice's Adventures in Wonderland* (1865; films: 1951, 1988, 2010), *The Lion, the Witch and the Wardrobe* (1950; film: 2005); *The Lord of the Rings* (1954-55; films: 2002-3), *Northern Lights* (1995; film: 2007 [*The Golden Compass*]) and *Harry Potter* (1997-2007; films: 2001-11). Prepare to discuss British children's books and their adaptations.

Chapter 2

Gender in the UK:
LGBT Issues

映画『マイ・ビューティフル・ランドレット』(1985)より

Warming-Up Activities:

1. Brainstorming on the Topic

ゲイやレズビアンの権利について知っていますか？　このような人々は、日本ではどのような境遇にあり、どのように見られていますか？

2. Vocabulary

☐ register	他動 (物を)登録する；自動 (for ～に)登録する	☐ acquaint	他動 ～を(with…に)精通させる
☐ vow	名 誓い、誓約	☐ reputation	名 名声、評判
☐ offence	名 犯罪、侮辱、攻撃(米 offense)	☐ threaten	他動 ～を脅かす、脅す(名 threat)
☐ launch	他動 (事業など)を始める	☐ regardless of	～に関係なく、～にかまわず
☐ prospect	名 見込み、可能性	☐ contribute	自動 (to ～に)貢献する、寄付する

Reading

The Marriage (Same Sex Couples) Act became law in England and Wales in July, 2013. By mid-March, 2014, couples were allowed to register their intent to marry, and shortly after the stroke of midnight on March 29 the first same-sex couples in the United Kingdom exchanged marriage vows. However, less than fifty years earlier homosexuality was still a criminal offence punishable by imprisonment. It was not until 1967 that homosexuality was decriminalised in the United Kingdom under the Sexual Offenses Act. As might be expected, 1967 also marked the beginning of an outpouring of British films pushing the boundaries of movie content by dealing more directly with LGBT (lesbian, gay, bisexual, transgendered) issues.

The past half century has seen the release of such films as *Sunday Bloody Sunday* (1971) with its love triangle plot involving a bisexual man and his male and female lovers; *My Beautiful Laundrette* (1985), a Thatcher-era inter-racial, gay romance; Sally Potter's *Orlando* (1992) starring Tilda Swinton as the time-travelling, sex-changing Orlando; and *Lilting* (2014) which, like *My Beautiful Laundrette*, combines gender issues with those of ethnicity and culture. In *Lilting*, the unexpected death of a young man brings his Chinese-Cambodian immigrant mother and his gay, white lover together as they struggle to deal with their loss. The mother's lack of English is as much a barrier between the two as is the boyfriend's homosexuality. In response to this growing body of LGBT-themed films, the British Film Institute launched its London Lesbian and Gay Film Festival (LLGFF) in 1986 (changed in 2014 to the more inclusively titled BFI Flare: London LGBT Film Festival).

A notable exception to the post-1967 proliferation of LGBT-themed British films is *Victim* (1961). Released six years prior to the 1967 Sexual Offences Act, *Victim* comes across in hindsight as a plea for the decriminalisation

映画『日曜日は別れの時』（1971）より

of homosexuality. [A] *Victim* stars Dirk Bogarde as Melville Farr, an up-and-coming London barrister soon to be honoured with the rank of Queen's Counsel and <u>deemed</u> a likely prospect for a judgeship in the near future. [B] Except for one problem: Melville Farr is homosexual. [C] Farr remains safely closeted until Jack, a young gay man he has become acquainted with, commits suicide as a result of being blackmailed by someone who knew of his homosexuality. Rather than endanger Farr's reputation and career, Jack hangs himself. [D] When Farr discovers why Jack has killed himself and that other members of London's gay community are being similarly threatened, he is determined to find the blackmailer regardless of the personal cost to himself.

Victim treats the topic of homosexuality directly while presenting competing reactions, ranging from the homophobic ("Why can't he stick with his own sort?") to the sympathetic ("Someone once called this law against homosexuality the blackmailer's charter.") to the personal ("I can't help the way I am, but the law says I'm a criminal."). Nor does it try to romanticise or sidestep the power of sexual attraction. When Farr's wife (unaware of the growing attraction that Farr was feeling) persists in questioning why he stopped seeing Jack, Farr finally tells her the truth: "I stopped seeing him because I wanted him. Do you understand? Because I *wanted* him!" It is even possible that *Victim*'s nonjudgmental but direct treatment of its theme contributed to the public's changing opinion and played some small part in the decriminalisation of homosexuality.

Notes

● l. 1: **The Marriage (Same Sex Couples) Act** 婚姻（同性婚）法 ● l. 5: **imprisonment** 名 投獄、禁固刑 ● l. 6: **decriminalised > decriminalise** 他動 ～を犯罪でないようにする（名 **decriminalisation**） ● l. 7: **outpouring** 名 流出、ほとばしり ● l. 9: **transgendered** 形 トランスジェンダーの ● l. 12: **interracial** 形 異人種間の ● l. 19: **the British Film Institute** 英国映画協会 ● l. 24: **proliferation** 名 増殖、急増 ● l. 25: **prior to** ～より前に ● l. 25-26: **the 1967 Sexual Offences Act** 1967年の性犯罪法 ● l. 27: **in hindsight** 後知恵で考えると ● l. 27: **plea** 名 嘆願、請願 ● l. 29: **barrister** 名 法廷弁護士 ● l. 29: **Queen's Counsel** 勅撰弁護士（国家元首が男性の場合は King's Counsel となる） ● l. 30: **judgeship** 名 裁判官の地位 ● l. 31: **closeted > closet** 他動 ～を閉じ込める、伏せておく ● l. 33: **endanger** 他動 ～を危険にさらす ● l. 38: **homophobic** 形 同性愛者を嫌悪する ● l. 41: **romanticise** 他動 ～をロマンティックにする ● l. 41: **sidestep** 他動 ～をよける ● l. 45: **nonjudgmental** 形 個人的基準に基づいた判断を避ける、偏向のない

Comprehension

1. What does the author imply about the 1967 Sexual Offenses Act?
    (A) It encouraged the making of LGBT-themed movies.
    (B) It discouraged the making of LGBT-themed movies.
    (C) It had no effect on the making of LGBT-themed movies.
    (D) It was passed due to the influence of LGBT-themed movies.

2. According to the essay, which of the following statements is TRUE regarding the Marriage (Same Sex Couples) Act?
    (A) Initially, it applied to only England.
    (B) It decriminalised homosexuality.
    (C) It allowed same sex couples to marry.
    (D) It has been the law for almost 50 years.

3. The expression shortly after the stroke of midnight in paragraph 1 is closest in meaning to
    (A) 11: 59 pm
    (B) 12: 01 am
    (C) 12:30 am
    (D) 1:00 am

4. The author cites the films *My Beautiful Laundrette* and *Lilting* as examples of
    (A) films that focus on gay romance.
    (B) films made before homosexuality was decriminalised.
    (C) films that combine gender and cultural issues.
    (D) films promoted by the British Film Institute.

5. The word body in paragraph 2 is closest in meaning to
    (A) figure
    (B) area
    (C) association
    (D) collection

6. According to the essay, all of the following are true about Melville Farr EXCEPT for:
   (A) He is being blackmailed.
   (B) He is a successful lawyer.
   (C) He may become a judge.
   (D) He is a homosexual man.

7. It is implied in the essay that Farr decides to find the blackmailer because
   (A) it is part of his job as a lawyer.
   (B) no one else is capable of doing it.
   (C) he feels responsible for Jack's death.
   (D) he is worried about his reputation and career.

8. The word deemed in paragraph 3 is closest in meaning to
   (A) denied
   (B) considered
   (C) forced
   (D) mistaken

9. [A], [B], [C] and [D] indicate where the following sentence can be added to paragraph 3. Mark your answer on your answer sheet.
   Financially well off and married to a beautiful woman who adores him, life looks good for Mr Farr.

10. The essay implies movies such as Victim
    (A) can help bring about social change.
    (B) have little effect on public opinion.
    (C) appeal primarily to gay audiences.
    (D) would probably not be made today.

Summary

Read the sentences below and choose the statement that best summarises the main idea of paragraph 3.

(A) *Victim* is typical of how British films treated homosexuality in the early 1960s.

(B) *Victim* is noteworthy for its accurate depiction of the British legal system.

(C) *Victim* is significant for its pre-1967 sympathetic portrayal of homosexuality.

Discussion

1. Based on your reading of the essay, discuss how thinking about gender has changed in Britain over the past fifty years. Do you feel the author provides an accurate account of the issue? Draw on your knowledge of films, current events or novels to support your view.

2. What are some issues regarding gender and LGBT rights in Japan? After reading the essay, how do you think Japan compares with Britain on these issues? Give examples to support your view.

Homework / Research

Watch the movie *Victim* (available on DVD). How do you feel about its portrayal of homosexuality? Do you find the characters believable? Do you agree with Farr's decision to pursue the blackmailer? You may also want to watch one or more of the other films mentioned in the essay and prepare a short oral report or presentation for class. For a larger selection of LGBT-themed films, go to the British Film Institute's homepage: http://www.bfi.org.uk

Chapter 3

Queen's English, Prince's English

ロンドンにあるバッキンガム宮殿

Warming-Up Activities:

1. Brainstorming on the Topic

イギリス標準発音は RP (Received Pronunciation) というが、これはよく Queen's English とも呼ばれる。イギリスの王室について知っていることを英語で書き出してみよう。

2. Vocabulary

☐ adopt	他動 ～を採り入れる	☐ vowel	他動 母音(cf. diphthong 二重母音)
☐ pronunciation	名 発音(他動 pronounce)	☐ merge	自動 (into/with ～に)溶け込む
☐ upbringing	名 育ち、子供のしつけ	☐ deliberately	副 意図的に(形 deliberate)
☐ aristocrat	名 貴族	☐ colloquial	形 口語的な、くだけた
☐ prestigious	形 名声のある、一流の	☐ modify	他動 ～を修正する

Reading

"But I can see the world has changed," says Queen Elizabeth II towards the end of the film, *The Queen* (2006), "And one must modernise." Indeed, the verb *modernise* is one of the key words of the film. The death of Princess Diana marked the advent of a new era with the term the then Prime Minister Tony Blair coined, "the People's Princess." Diana Spencer got married to Prince Charles in 1981 and got divorced in 1996, after they found out they both had extramarital relationships. Besides this scandal, she was very popular for her media presence and her charity work including her visits to orphanages and AIDS treatment centres across the world. She was no longer an HRH when she died in a car crash in Paris in 1997. As in the film, the British Royals treated her death as a "private matter" at first. They did not understand she remained a "princess"—or "the People's Princess", as Blair put it—in British people's mind. People wanted to have a public funeral and began to criticise the Queen and the Royal Family. The Queen finally decided to adopt this "modern" idea. However, this is not the only kind of modernisation that has taken place in the Royal Family since the 1980s. Their language has also changed.

Queen's English—or RP (Received Pronunciation), as it is called—has been arguably the hallmark of good upbringing and education and the cornerstone of the English language for many years. RP is a standard accent of English based on aristocrats' speech in south-east England. [A] It is associated with British aristocrats, upper-class people and public school graduates—a public school being a prestigious independent school for upper-class and upper-middle-class children. [B] Both English and foreign actors and actresses try to imitate this accent when they play English upper-class characters or European royals. [C] Technically speaking, Queen's English is often regarded as a slightly more traditional accent. [D] In the 1950s, Queen Elizabeth II used a mid-open front vowel for the near-open front vowel. Therefore, her "land" sounded like "lend". She used—and still uses—a shorter open back vowel in *lot* and a longer mid-open back vowel in *cloth*, although the latter vowel has merged into the former in RP since the beginning of the 20th century. Despite these differences, Queen's English has long been identified with RP and regarded as a standard.

ウィリアム王子の家族

The son of the People's Princess, Prince William, on the other hand, prefers a more <u>plebeian</u> variation of English, even though he often reveals his royal origins—perhaps against his will—in his speech. He deliberately chooses "common" vocabulary. In the first televised interview with Prince William and his fiancée Catherine Middleton (on Sky News, 16 November 2010), he observed, "as any guy out there will know, it takes a certain amount of motivation to get yourself going." Everyone knows Prince William is not just "any guy out there," but he tries to identify himself with everyman. So, he uses "any guy out there", instead of a more formal expression. Later in this interview, he described their temperamental difference as "<u>different characters and stuff</u>", using the colloquial *stuff* at the end. Also, he imitates young London-based "modified RP" speakers' accent at times. "Modified RP" is a collective term for various accents based on RP that preserve local colours. A word-end plosive is pronounced with a glottal stop. "I was planning it and then it just felt really right out in Africa," says he, sounding a bit like "I was planning i' and then i' just felt really righ' ou' in Africa." Even though he sounds "posh", the People's Princess' son probably wants to be the People's Prince.

Notes

● l. 4 : **coined** > **coin**　他動　〜を創り出す　● l. 6 : **extramarital**　形　婚外の　● l. 8 : **orphanages** > **orphanage**　名　孤児院　● l. 9 : **HRH**　閣下、閣下と呼ばれる身分の人 (= His Royal Highness または Her Royal Highness の略）　● l. 17 : **hallmark**　名　品質証明、保証をするもの　● l. 17 : **cornerstone**　名　基礎　● l. 25 : **mid-open front vowel**　前舌半広母音（発音記号 /ɛ/）　● l. 25 : **near-open front vowel**　前舌狭めの広母音（発音記号 /æ/）　● l. 26 : **open back vowel**　後舌広母音（発音記号 /ɒ/）　● l. 26-27 : **mid-open back vowel**　後舌半広母音（発音記号 /ɔ/）　● l. 42 : **temperamental**　形　気質の　● l. 45 : **plosive**　名　破裂音　● l. 45 : **glottal stop**　声門閉鎖音（発音記号 /ʔ/）

Chapter 3　▶　15

Comprehension

1. By "one must modernise", Queen Elizabeth II means that they must
   (A) install new equipment.
   (B) demand something new or unusual.
   (C) restore something old to a good state.
   (D) embrace a new idea or method.

2. The word advent in paragraph 1 is closest in meaning to
   (A) arrival
   (B) departure
   (C) heyday
   (D) primetime

3. Princess Diana was no longer an HRH because
   (A) she lost her title by her divorce.
   (B) she wasn't faithful to her divorced husband.
   (C) she committed adultery.
   (D) she was killed in a traffic accident.

4. [A], [B], [C] and [D] indicate where the following sentences can be added to paragraph 2. Mark the answer on your answer sheet.
   In *Roman Holiday* (1953), Audrey Hepburn (half-British, half-Dutch) speaks RP to fit the role of Princess Ann, even though the nationality of this fictional princess is unknown. She pronounces "Rome" rather like "Reum"—the first element of the diphthong being unrounded in traditional RP.

5. According to paragraph 2, all of the following statements are true EXCEPT
   (A) English peers speak RP
   (B) Rich factory owners in England also speak RP
   (C) Certain RP vowels sounds differently in Queen Elizabeth II's speech
   (D) RP speakers use the same vowel for the words *lot* and *cloth*

6. The word <u>arguably</u> in paragraph 2 indicates that the author
   (A) does not believe what he writes in the rest of the sentence
   (B) is really sure that his statement is true
   (C) admits that some people disagree with him or her
   (D) is fully aware that he is disapproving of a widely-held belief

7. The word <u>accent</u> in paragraph 2 is closest in meaning to
   (A) importance
   (B) emphasis
   (C) stress
   (D) dialect

8. The word <u>plebeian</u> in paragraph 3 is closest in meaning to
   (A) accustomed
   (B) common
   (C) enigmatic
   (D) generous

9. The phrase <u>different characters and stuff</u> in paragraph 3 can be best replaced by
   (A) different persons and materials
   (B) different temperaments and so on
   (C) different mentalities by all means
   (D) different individuals et cetera

10. According to paragraph 3, Prince William
    (A) does not speak the same variation of English as his grandmother.
    (B) loves local colours.
    (C) avoids using young people's colloquialisms.
    (D) makes every effort to sound upper-class.

Summary

Read the sentences below and choose the statement that best summarises paragraph 3.

(A) Prince William tries to sound like a common man, even though it is difficult for him.

(B) Because of his effort, Prince William remains the People's Prince in British people's mind.

(C) "Modified RP" is the variation of English Prince William speaks.

Discussion

1. How would you compare the essay with recent films, novels, newspaper articles or webpages concerning the British Royal Family? Do they provide similar pictures or very different pictures?

2. "Queen's English should always be the cornerstone of standard English"—do you agree or disagree? Provide reasons to support your argument.

Homework / Research

Find out more on the British Royal Family. Read articles on the death of Princess Diana, the documentary film *Unlawful Killing* (2011), Prince Charles' marriage to Camilla or Prince William's marriage to Catherine, or novels such as *The Queen and I* (1992) and *Queen Camilla* (2006). Watch films such as *The Queen* (2006) and *Diana* (2013). Prepare to discuss the changing images of the British Royal Family.

Chapter 4

Class and the British Way of Life

映画『蜜の味』(1961)より

Warming-Up Activities:

1. Brainstorming on the Topic

日本で、所得や財産、学歴、性別や出身地は、個人の社会における立場やステータスを決めるのにどのような役割を果たしているのだろう？ イギリスや他の国で階級という言葉で表現されるものについて何か知っていることはあるだろうか？ 階級が違うと何が違うのだろう？

2. Vocabulary

☐ uniquely	副 特有の形で(形 unique)	☐ affluent	形 裕福な(名 affluence)
☐ trait	名 特徴	☐ be composed of	〜で構成されている
☐ obsession	名 強迫観念(他動 obsess)	☐ fascinate	他動 〜を魅了する
☐ consensus	名 意見の一致、コンセンサス	☐ optimism	名 楽観主義(形 optimistic)
☐ current	形 現在の	☐ industrial	形 工業の、工場の(名 industry)

Reading

Upper-, middle- and lower-class: all are terms used to describe social membership in Britain. Of course, classes such as these exist in all societies, but many people think that class is a uniquely British trait. While talking about class is something of a British obsession, there is no consensus about its shape or meaning. The most recent effort to shed light on class was conducted in 2011 by the BBC and sociologists from Britain and Europe using an online audience of more than 160,000 people. Not only do the results of the survey suggest that the current understanding is unrealistic; they also point to seven distinct classes in today's Britain.

Class, the researchers say, is not just based on jobs and salary but on a combination of economic, cultural and social factors, or capital. A group called the Elite are at the top of British society, holding the greatest amount of economic, cultural and social capital. Beneath them is the Established Middle Class, lower down the Working Class. At the very bottom are the poor, or what the researchers call the Precariat, living the most impoverished lives of all UK citizens. Surprisingly, only 39 percent of Britons follow clearly middle- and working-class lifestyles while a significant number of people can be found in new social formations: the Technical Middle Class, high in economic capital but low in cultural and social connections, and the New Affluent Workers and Emergent Service Workers, both composed predominantly of young Britons.

Britons at the lower end of the class system have fascinated British filmmakers. A "new wave" of social realism, beginning with *Room at the Top* (1959), offered an honest exploration of working-class characters and the promise of affluence. [A] In *Look Back in Anger* (1959), working-class Jimmy Porter is denied opportunities despite his university education. [B] Porter's caring middle-class wife Alison suffers much of his resentment. [C] *A Taste of Honey* (1961) follows Jo, a 17-year-old working-class girl who becomes pregnant with the child of a black sailor and rooms with a gay student who offers to marry her until she can find someone to love. [D]

Of course, such films explored class experience in the 1950s and 60s when affluence was growing in Britain. Recent films record a more desperate world, namely the world of the Precariat. While some of these new films, such as *Brighton Rock* (2010) and *NEDs* (2010), show tragic characters trapped by poverty, violence and despair, others provide a realistic view of social and economic forces in the new global order. Set in Glasgow in the 1970s *NEDs* (or non-educated delinquents) follows a talented working-class boy named John McGill who cannot escape family and gang violence. *It's a Free World* (2007), on the other hand, has a clear message about the political, social and economic forces affecting British people at the lower end of society. A more subtle exploration of class is *Happy-Go-Lucky* (2008), in which a kind-hearted primary school teacher discovers the class resentment and bigotry of her driving instructor. The most bleak of recent films about class is *The Selfish Giant* (2013), which takes its title from a Christian fable by 19th-century author Oscar Wilde. In so doing, it recalls the deep class inequality of Wilde's time but contains none of his optimism about better lives for the lower classes. *The Selfish Giant* is set in the northern industrial district of Bradford, and follows the lives of Arbor and Swifty, youth from families on the brink of collapse. A man named Kitten is the owner of the scrapyard who pushes the desperate boys into theft or involves them in his gambling schemes. Whereas Wilde's selfish giant renounces his evil ways, Kitten exploits the children without mercy until the death of one of them brings about his arrest.

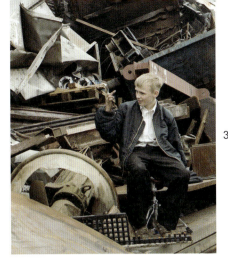

映画『わがままな大男』(2013)より

Notes

- l. 11-12: **economic, cultural and social capital** 経済資本、文化資本および社会関係資本（フランスの社会学者 Pierre Bourdieu によると、資本には経済的なもの［資産］だけではなく、マナーや言葉遣いや音楽の趣味などの文化資本や、貴族や地方の名士とのコネクションなどの社会関係資本も含まれる）
- l. 14: **impoverished** 形 貧しい、極貧の
- l. 24: **resentment** 名 憤り
- l. 34: **Glasgow** グラスゴー（スコットランドの工業都市）
- l. 35: **delinquent** 名 非行少年、義務不履行者
- l. 40: **bigotry** 名 偏狭さ、偏狭な言動（人は bigot）
- l. 44: **Bradford** ブラッドフォード（イングランド北部の工業都市、現在はパキスタン系移民が多い）
- l. 45: **on the brink of** 〜に瀕して
- l. 47: **Whereas** 接 〜の一方で
- l. 47: **renounces > renounce** 他動 〜を放棄する、断念する

Comprehension

1. In paragraph 1, the author claims that
   - (A) The class system in the UK has remained relatively the same.
   - (B) The BBC has played an important role in shaping class in the UK.
   - (C) Class is important in the UK but it is not well understood.
   - (D) Class is unique to the UK.

2. Which of the statements about films that deal with class is true?
   - (A) They are all realistic and pessimistic in their depictions of class.
   - (B) Most are set in the northern industrial districts of Britain.
   - (C) These films all feature characters tragically trapped by poverty and violence.
   - (D) Recent films reflect the economic desperation of many in the UK today.

3. The phrase on the brink of collapse in paragraph 4 is closest in meaning to
   - (A) nearly broken
   - (B) fallen down
   - (C) in between jobs
   - (D) close to ruin

4. Which of the following facts is NOT true according to the passage?
   - (A) One recent survey claims there are three main class groupings in the UK.
   - (B) Less than half of Britons have middle- or working-class lifestyles.
   - (C) Britons talk very much about class.
   - (D) The Elite have the largest amount of social, cultural and economic resources at their disposal.

5. The phrase In so doing in paragraph 4 refers to
   - (A) the titling of the film
   - (B) the bleakness of the film
   - (C) the Christian aspects of the film
   - (D) the optimism of the film

6. The phrase <u>uniquely British trait</u> in paragraph 1 is closest in meaning to
   (A) a British fact
   (B) a characteristically UK phenomenon
   (C) a characteristic of England
   (D) the treatment of class in the UK

7. [A], [B], [C] and [D] indicate where the following sentence can be added to paragraph 3. Mark the answer on your answer sheet.
   In this film, class anger takes on a distinctly misogynistic tone.

8. According to the passage, films about class can be broken down into which two categories?
   (A) Tragic and comic
   (B) Realistic and melodramatic
   (C) Films that deal with affluence and those that deal with poverty
   (D) Tragic and socially realistic

9. Which of the following claims is NOT made in the essay?
   (A) Some people think that class is a characteristic part of British culture and society.
   (B) The situation of working people and the poor is a topic that has emerged only in recent years in British films.
   (C) The British new wave dealt with working class characters in an honest fashion.
   (D) Class position is influenced by a number of factors.

10. Which of claims about films that deal with class is true?
    (A) Some films treat lower-class characters as tragically unable to escape their situation.
    (B) Class has not been dealt with extensively in British cinema.
    (C) Many films show that class can be transcended, that a classless society is possible.
    (D) A number of films suggest that socialism can solve problems of class discrimination.

Summary

Read the sentences below and choose the sentence that best summarises paragraph 2.

(A) Members of the elite are at the top of the social structure.

(B) Not so many people as before follow middle- or working-class lifestyles.

(C) Class is complex and there is a variety of groupings in Britain today.

Discussion

1. Discuss the concept of social, cultural and economic capital. What specific resources do you think the researchers have in mind for each of these factors?

2. What are the implications of a film that shows class in tragic terms? Can realist films serve social progress? What differentiates a film that merely exploits class for dramatic effect and one that attempts to further social progress?

Homework / Research

1. Director Clio Barnard has stated that Oscar Wilde's children's story has influenced her film only superficially. Read Wilde's "The Selfish Giant" and assess this judgment, discussing the similarities and differences between the story and the film.

2. Watch one or more of the British new wave films, including *Room at the Top* (1959), *Look Back in Anger* (1959), *Saturday Night and Sunday Morning* (1960), *A Taste of Honey* (1961) and *This Sporting Life* (1963), and prepare to discuss the representation of working-class life. Do these films depict people's lives in a realistic way? Explain with examples.

Chapter 5

Football and Language

サッカーの聖地、ウェンブリー・スタジアム

Warming-Up Activities:

1. Brainstorming on the Topic

イギリスにおいて、サッカー(football)はとても大きな意味を持っている。大きなビジネスであるだけでなく、文化として根付いている。イギリスのサッカー選手やサッカーについて知っていることを英語で書き出してみよう。

2. Vocabulary

☐ stereotype	名 ステレオタイプ	☐ refer to	～に言及する、(+as...)～を…と呼ぶ
☐ strategy	名 戦術	☐ involve	他動 ～を関わらせる
☐ opportunity	名 機会	☐ procedure	名 手続き
☐ accent	名 訛り (cf. dialect)	☐ appropriate	形 適切な
☐ describe	他動 ～を描写する、記述する	☐ illustrate	他動 ～を例証する

Reading

"Nobody expects a footballer to have any kind of an IQ," said Frank Lampard in an interview in 2010, "which is a bit of an unfair stereotype." The English midfielder has an IQ score of 150, high enough for Mensa, was educated at a prestigious independent school and got an A star and three As in his GCSEs. Naturally, all his teachers wanted him to go to university. A high IQ is, however, not what we usually expect from a footballer. At least not in England. Despite the complexity of modern football strategies, most English fans appreciate footballers' toughness rather than their cleverness. Old-fashioned fans hate those strikers who try to earn a penalty with a "dive" in the box.* Nowhere is football more strongly associated with machismo than in England. Besides, footballers rarely sound very intelligent. Most professional footballers start their careers in a local football academy after finishing school, so they don't usually receive higher education. Even if a footballer has Lampard's IQ, he has little, if any, opportunity to study at a higher level or even learn to speak like an educated person. Indeed, Lampard is an unassuming, plain-spoken man, who has an Essex accent. In England, educated upper- and middle-class people speak RP, a standard accent of British English.

練習中のフランク・ランパード選手

There is even a comedy sketch about the gap between footballers and football pundits. In a Monty Python sketch, a snobbish football critic interviews a typical footballer, making an ostensible display of his mastery of literary and philosophical language. He begins the interview this way: "Last night in the Stadium of Light, Jarrow, we witnessed the resuscitation of a great footballing tradition, when Jarrow United came of age, in a European sense, with an almost Proustian display of modern existentialist football, virtually annihilating by midfield moral argument the now surely obsolescent *catenaccio* defensive philosophy of Signor Alberto Fanffino." This is hilarious because we don't normally describe modern football as "existentialist" or "Proustian". We often talk about football "philosophy" or "style", but it is about the team's or the coach's preference for certain strategies (e.g. "short-passing football" and "counter-attacking football"). Even if players switch their positions and therefore do not play their nominal roles, we just call it a "fluid system". We don't cite it as an example of existence that precedes essence. Nor do we discuss "moral argument" in the midfield. Also, the critic's use of Latinate words such as "resuscitation" is sharply contrasted by the artlessness of the footballer, who keeps saying "Good evening, Brian" and "I'm opening a boutique", not understanding the critic's questions.

Footballers may not understand some of the pundits' snobbish language, but footballers' language has seeped into common parlance. We may begin a meeting by saying, "Let's *kick off* the meeting". A "kick off" is the start of a football match. When someone is observing a situation but trying not to be involved, he or she is "watching from the sidelines". Assistant referees always watch from the sidelines, but they should not be involved in the game. We should not change the conditions of a process while in progress, just as we should not move the goalposts. If you see someone doing it, you may well shout, "Don't *move the goalposts*!" These expressions are very casual and therefore not appropriate in a formal document, but they are easily understood by people from all walks of life in England. This is another example to illustrate the nationwide popularity of the sport.

* A penalty kick is awarded when the opponent team's player commits a foul in his own penalty area.

Notes

- l. 2: **midfielder** 名 ミッドフィールダー（サッカーのポジションで、中盤のこと） ● l. 3: **Mensa** メンサ（IQテスト高得点者のみが加入できる国際社交組織） ● l. 4: **GCSEs** 中等教育修了試験（General Certificate of Secondary Education、第6章で詳述） ● l. 16: **sketch** 名 コント ● l. 19: **ostensible** 形 これみよがしな ● l. 22: **Jarrow** イングランド北東部の都市（実際には Jarrow にプロ・サッカー・チームはない） ● l. 23: **Proustian** 形 プルースト的な（Proust はフランスの小説家） ● l. 24: **existentialist** 形 実存主義の 名 実存主義者 ● l. 25: **obsolescent** 形 廃れている ● l. 25: ***catenaccio*** カテナチオ（守備的なサッカーの戦術） ● l. 25: **Signor Alberto Fanffino** 架空のイタリア人監督 ● l. 26: **hilarious** 形 滑稽な ● l. 31: **existence that precedes essence** 「本質に先立つ存在」（実存主義哲学において、名前や性別といった「本質」よりも個人の存在が先立つものとされる） ● l. 34: **Latinate** 形 ラテン語由来の ● l. 34: **boutique** 名 店（ここではブティックの意味ではない）

Comprehension

1. According to the passage, all of the following statements are true of Frank Lampard EXCEPT
    (A) He studied at a highly selective school.
    (B) He was good enough at academic subjects to study at university.
    (C) He performed very well in the IQ test.
    (D) He always talks like a scholar.

2. According to the passage, which of the following statements is true of most English football fans?
    (A) They love smart players with high IQ scores.
    (B) They are all familiar with the newest strategies.
    (C) They admire players' physical strength.
    (D) They don't dive in the penalty area.

3. According to the passage, most professional English footballers
    (A) go to university before playing for a famous club.
    (B) never go to an independent school.
    (C) study academic subjects very hard at a special college.
    (D) play for a youth team after graduating from school.

4. The word pundits in paragraph 2 is closest in meaning to
    (A) experts
    (B) managers
    (C) priests
    (D) servants

5. The word language in paragraph 2 is closest in meaning to
    (A) communication
    (B) discussion
    (C) presentation
    (D) terminology

6. The word resuscitation in paragraph 2 is closest in meaning to
   (A) recommendation
   (B) revelation
   (C) revitalisation
   (D) revolution

7. According to paragraph 2, which of the following can be classified as the coach's "philosophy" or "style" of football?
   (A) He believes men should work outside and women should do housework.
   (B) He always tells his defenders to send a long ball to the target man.
   (C) He doesn't care whether he is nominated for the best player of the year.
   (D) He openly criticises the opponent's nuclear energy policy.

8. In the Monty Python sketch mentioned in paragraph 2, the footballer supposedly feels
   (A) really angry.
   (B) mildly amused.
   (C) extremely delighted.
   (D) utterly confused.

9. The phrase seeped into common parlance in paragraph 3 is closest in meaning to
   (A) become known to ordinary citizens
   (B) drawn more and more attention
   (C) entered our everyday conversation
   (D) fallen short of our expectations

10. According to paragraph 3, all of the following statements are true EXCEPT:
    (A) The phrase "watch from the sidelines" may be used to describe a person who tries to grasp the situation but does not try to change it.
    (B) A boss who changes the signed contract in his favour may be criticised for "moving the goalposts".
    (C) You can use phrases like "watch from the sidelines" in a letter of consent.
    (D) English people know what you mean by "moving the goalposts", regardless of their social origins.

Summary

Read the sentences below and choose the statement that best summarises paragraph 2.

(A) Monty Python's sketch shows that it is hard for footballers to get on well with football pundits in reality.

(B) As in a Monty Python sketch, modern football resembles existentialist philosophy because existence precedes essence.

(C) Football pundits' snobbery, as well as footballers' ignorance, is caricatured in a Monty Python sketch.

Discussion

1. How would you compare British images of footballers and Japanese (or American, etc.) images of footballers? Are they similar or different? In what way? What about football critics?

2. In England, language (vocabulary as well as accents) often serves as a "class marker" (that reveals the speaker's own social background). What do you know about language and class in England? Is it true of Japanese society?

Homework / Research

Find out more on British sports and culture. Watch films such as *Fever Pitch* (1997), *My Name Is Joe* (1998), *Purely Belter* (2000), *Bend It Like Beckham* (2002), *Green Street* (2005) and *The Damned United* (2009). Alternatively, you can work on other sports in Britain (e.g. cricket, tennis, horse race). Prepare to discuss the ways footballers and football fans are represented in the media.

Chapter 6

Education in Britain

映画『ヒストリー・ボーイズ』(2006)より

Warming-Up Activities:

1. Brainstorming on the Topic

『ハリー・ポッター』のシリーズはホグワーツ魔法学校を舞台としている。全寮制で、科目を自ら選択して受講する。7年制で、5年目には大きな試験がある。このように、イギリスの教育制度は日本とではずいぶん異なる。イギリスの教育制度について知っていることやキーワードを英語で書き出してみよう。

2. Vocabulary

☐ rebel	名 反逆者 自動 反逆する	☐ focus	自動 (on ～に)集中する
☐ encourage	他動 ～を励ます、促す	☐ resemblance	名 類似点(他動 resemble)
☐ reflect	他動 ～を反映する	☐ compel	他動 ～に強いる、(to do...)に…させる
☐ reform	名 (政治などの)改革	☐ controversial	形 物議を醸す(名 controversy)
☐ prohibit	他動 ～を禁止する	☐ authority	名 権威、当局

Reading

We often say, "Everybody loves rebels." Indeed, rebels are often favourably portrayed in British novels, plays, films and comedy sketches set in secondary schools. Harry Potter, the eponymous hero of the series, is often left with no choice but to break the school rules, whilst Albus Dumbledore, the headmaster, often encourages him to do whatever he thinks is right rather than always abide by the rules. Needless to say, that does not mean British schools are dens of rebels. Rather, it reflects what people dream of becoming but choose not to be.

Recent films often centre on rebellious teachers. They are not just rebellious, but they rebel against certain educational "reforms", or more precisely, British Prime Minister Margaret Thatcher's educational "reforms". This trend is exemplified by the Harry Potter series and Alan Bennett's play *The History Boys* (2004)—and its film version (2006).

Margaret Thatcher adopted a "free-market" approach to education. She introduced the National Curriculum, detailing what subjects to be taught at what age, and the "league tables" or the ranking of all secondary schools based on the students' GCSE and A-level results. [A] In England and Wales, children enter a secondary school at the age of 11 (for state schools) and take the exams called GCSE (General Certificate of Secondary Education) in core subjects (English, maths and science) and a choice of other subjects at 16 on the completion of secondary education. [B] Those who wish to study at university proceed to the "sixth form", two years of additional schooling, to prepare for examinations A-level examinations—now in two parts, AS (Advanced Subsidiary Level) and A2 (Advanced Level)—to enter a university of their choice. After Thatcher's reforms, state schools make every effort to gain a better position in the league tables. [C] The GCSEs have been the subject of heated debate over the past decade, but the government will not likely give up the free-market approach. [D]

映画『ヒストリー・ボーイズ』(2006) より

These changes have invited criticism. In *Harry Potter and the Order of the Phoenix* (2003), Dolores Umbridge, sent from the Ministry of Magic, prohibits students from practising magic and orders them to focus on the exams—"OWLs" in the wizarding world—citing the importance of "accountability" in her speech. The reference is more explicit in the film adaptation (2007), where the actress' hairstyle bears a resemblance to the former prime minister's. Dumbledore rebels against her and wins the reader's trust. In *The History Boys*, the general studies teacher Hector takes a very traditional approach to teaching, hoping to enrich his students' intellectual lives and inspire them to be "well-rounded" persons. A young history teacher, Irwin, on the other hand, takes a new, overly exam-oriented approach as if to pander to the government's policy. He is the favourite of the headmaster, who feels compelled to send very good students to Oxford to have a better position in the league tables. Ironically, the play reveals Irwin's rebelliousness, too. He encourages his students to answer exam questions in apparently controversial ways and spice up their answers by adding "gobbets" or quotes from literary masterpieces. He believes students should invert an officially accepted theory to attract the examiners of Oxford and Cambridge, as if one should rebel against authority to make it to the top. Besides, he advises his students to recycle in a new way what they have learned in Hector's class. In this respect, Irwin revitalises traditional teaching.

Important notice: you should not confuse fiction with reality. British schools are no more heavily staffed by rebels than by witches and wizards. We take vicarious pleasure in identifying with rebels in fiction instead of becoming ones ourselves.

Notes

- l. 2 : **secondary school** 中等学校(日本の中学校と高等学校を合わせたもの)
- l. 3 : **eponymous** 形 タイトルと同名の
- l. 4 : **headmaster** 名 校長(アメリカ英語の principal に当たる)
- l. 12 : **free-market** 市場経済の(名詞として使う場合、ハイフンを取る)
- l. 29 : **Ministry of Magic** 魔法省(ハリー・ポッター・シリーズに登場する架空の省庁)
- l. 30-31 : **wizarding world** 魔法界(ハリー・ポッター・シリーズではこのように表現されているが、一般的には magical world などを使う)
- l. 31 : **accountability** 名 説明責任
- l. 37 : **exam-oriented** 試験中心の(名詞 + -oriented で様々な形容詞が作れる)

Comprehension

1. The phrase abide by in paragraph 1 is closest in meaning to
    (A) adhere to
    (B) disagree with
    (C) invest in
    (D) speculate on

2. Which of the following facts can be inferred from the phrase Needless to say in paragraph 1?
    (A) It is not surprising that most students and teachers comply with regulations.
    (B) It is quite natural that not many students and teachers live in school premises.
    (C) Many people know British students and teachers are most rebellious.
    (D) It is rather odd that every student or teacher has the right to break school rules.

3. The phrase This trend in paragraph 2 refers to the fact that
    (A) Margaret Thatcher carried out educational reforms.
    (B) certain educational reforms go hand in hand with Thatcher's policy.
    (C) more and more movies feature teachers disagreeing with Thatcher's reforms.
    (D) Margaret Thatcher's educational reforms are glamorised in recent films.

4. According to paragraph 3, the following statements are true EXCEPT:
    (A) Secondary schools have been ranked since Thatcher's educational reforms.
    (B) Thatcher introduced the GCSE and A-level examinations.
    (C) In England, not all students are required to study at sixth-form college.
    (D) Many people have openly criticised the current GCSEs.

5. [A], [B], [C] and [D] indicate where the following sentence can be added to paragraph 3. Mark the answer on your answer sheet.
    Unfortunately, many of them try to increase their students' exam scores rather than the quality of education.

6. The word core in paragraph 3 is closest in meaning to
   (A) authentic
   (B) compulsory
   (C) elective
   (D) invariable

7. According to paragraph 4, which of the following statements is true?
   (A) Dolores Umbridge introduces the exams called "OWLs" in the wizarding world.
   (B) Dolores Umbridge is responsible for accountability at school.
   (C) Dolores Umbridge speaks more explicitly in the film than in the novel.
   (D) Dolores Umbridge has a similar hairstyle to Thatcher in the film.

8. According to paragraph 4, which of the following does Irwin most likely tell his students?
   (A) Life goes on and you may contribute a verse. What will your verse be?
   (B) You don't have to understand poetry now. I don't. But learn it now, know it now, and you will understand it.
   (C) I can't make you invisible, but I can make you blend in with the crowd.
   (D) Take Stalin, generally agreed to be a monster. Find something to say in his defence. Defend the indefensible.

9. A well-rounded person in paragraph 4 can be defined as someone who
   (A) has a rounded shape especially in the middle.
   (B) shows interest or has knowledge in many fields.
   (C) excels many people in traditional subjects such as Latin.
   (D) can easily adapt himself or herself to a new environment.

10. By take vicarious pleasure in identifying with rebels in fiction in paragraph 5, the author means
    (A) think seriously that we can relate to rebels in fiction.
    (B) want to become rebels in fiction if we can.
    (C) supposedly represent those who enjoy emulating rebels in fiction.
    (D) feel happy by imagining ourselves being rebels in fiction.

Summary

Read the sentences below and choose the statement that best summarises the passage.

(A) In Britain, teachers are becoming more and more vocal about Thatcher's educational reforms, as in recent British films.

(B) Recent British films feature those teachers who rebel against the free-market approach to education, which represents people's secret desire.

(C) *Harry Potter and the Order of the Phoenix* and *The History Boys* represent two opposite responses to Thatcher's educational reforms in Britain.

Discussion

1. How would you compare British secondary schools with Japanese ones? Are they similar or different? In what way? What about educational system?

2. How would you describe teachers like Dumbledore, Umbridge, Hector and Irwin? Whose approach/teaching philosophy do you appreciate most? Why?

Homework / Research

Find out more on secondary education in Britain. Read articles on public schools (independent schools) and GCSEs. Watch films such as *Goodbye, Mr. Chips* (1969), *Another Country* (1984), *If . . .* (1968), *Melody* (1971), *The History Boys* and *Harry Potter and the Order of the Phoenix*. Prepare to discuss the changing images of British secondary schools.

Chapter 7

World War I:
One Hundred Years After

第一次世界大戦の塹壕戦の様子

Warming-Up Activities:

1. Brainstorming on the Topic

第一次世界大戦について知っていることを言ってみよう。また、開戦100周年を記念してイベントが行われていることが、なぜ議論を呼んでいるのか考えてみよう。

2. Vocabulary

☐ declare	他動 ～を宣言する、布告する		☐ commemorate	他動 ～を記念する
☐ necessity	名 必要性		☐ dedicate	他動 ～を(to…に)捧げる
☐ involvement	名 関わり、関与		☐ evident	形 明白な
☐ insufficiently	副 不十分に (対 sufficiently)		☐ rational	形 合理的な
☐ patriotic	形 愛国的な (名 patriot, patriotism)		☐ accusation	名 告発 (他動 accuse)

Reading

TV番組『ブラックアダー』シーズン4（1989）より

On August 4, 1914, after Germany invaded Belgium, Britain in turn declared war on Germany. With the centenary of Britain's entry into World War I approaching, preparations are in full swing for an appropriately solemn yet memorable commemoration of the anniversary. British people are finding, though, that discussions of the meaning of "The Great War" and Britain's role in it can still become quite emotional and even divisive. In an interview with *The Washington Post*, David Reynolds, University of Cambridge history professor and author of *The Long Shadow: The Great War and the Twentieth Century*, notes that World War I for the British (like Vietnam for Americans) "is hard to present as a success, and explanations for why you got into it are not very satisfying".

Questioning the necessity of Britain's involvement in the war and focusing on the wholesale carnage, however, can be viewed as engaging in needless hand-wringing or, worse, being insufficiently patriotic regarding the memory of the almost one million fallen British troops. British Education Secretary Michael Gove, for example, has gone on record as stating that there is a "right way" to commemorate Britain's involvement in the war. For Gove and other like-minded citizens the "right way" necessitates viewing and teaching World War I as a costly but necessary and "just" war.

It comes as no surprise that Gove has been critical of depictions of World War I that are less than reverent. His views have been especially harsh toward movies such as *Oh! What a Lovely War* (1969) and the 1980s situation comedy, *Blackadder*. Gove went so far as to argue that the fourth series in particular of the popular television show

("Blackadder Goes Forth") should be banned from use in British schools because it promotes "left-wing myths" and depicts the First World War as a "misbegotten shambles".

Blackadder, starring Rowan Atkinson (of *Mr. Bean* fame) in the title role, was broadcast on BBC in the 1980s in four series set in different historical periods. "Blackadder Goes Forth" is set in the trenches of the Western Front at the height of the war. Atkinson's character, Captain Edmund Blackadder, though, is no self-sacrificing leader of men; rather, he is a self-serving schemer dedicated to devising ways to avoid battle by staying in the trenches; or, if he must leave the trenches, let it be for Paris or London and not the "no-man's-land" of the battlefield.

[A] The irreverent, iconoclastic nature of *Blackadder* is evident primarily through the cynical observations of Captain Blackadder, as when he notes that it "would be a damn sight simpler if we'd just stayed in England and shot fifty-thousand of our men a week". In the final episode, with a suicidal offensive looming, Blackadder attempts to explain what caused the war. Unable to provide a rational explanation, he finally settles for: "It was just too much effort not to have a war." [B] A more succinct, yet scathing, accusation of the failings of politicians and military leaders would be hard to find. Are such views unpatriotic? [C] The fact that an episode of a television sitcom can still spark volatile reactions twenty-five years after it first aired is evidence that the issue of Britain's role in World War I, even one-hundred years after it began, remains unsettled. [D]

Notes

- l. 10: **divisive** 形 争いの種になる、不和を生じさせる
- l. 11: **The Washington Post** ワシントン・ポスト（アメリカの高級紙）
- l. 25: **reverent** 形 敬虔な、うやうやしい
- l. 26: **situation comedy** シチュエーション・コメディー（sitcom とも）
- l. 33: **trenches > trench** 名 塹壕
- l. 35: **schemer** 名 陰謀を巡らせる人
- l. 43: **succinct** 形 簡潔な
- l. 43: **scathing** 形 痛烈な、容赦のない
- l. 46: **volatile** 形 揮発性の、（気分・性格・情勢などが）変わりやすい

Comprehension

1. According to the essay, how do the British feel about the First World War?
    (A) The war happened so long ago that no one really cares.
    (B) The war is seen as a necessary and worthwhile sacrifice.
    (C) The war is seen as clearly a waste of lives and money.
    (D) The war continues to be a controversial topic for the British.

2. According to the essay, which of the following statements is true about both David Reynolds and Michael Gove?
    (A) They both teaches history.
    (B) They are both interested in World War I.
    (C) They both wrote a book about World War I.
    (D) They are both fans of *Blackadder*.

3. The word Great in paragraph 1 is closest in meaning to
    (A) immense
    (B) splendid
    (C) famous
    (D) grand

4. The author cites the film *Oh! What a Lovely War* as an example of
    (A) David Reynolds' scholarly work as a historian.
    (B) what Michael Gove considers the "right way" to commemorate the war.
    (C) the kind of movie that Michael Gove would not approve of.
    (D) a movie featuring Rowan Atkinson's "Mr. Bean" character.

5. The expression It comes as no surprise in paragraph 3 is closest in meaning to
    (A) it is unexpected
    (B) it is not unexpected
    (C) it is no longer surprising
    (D) it has become surprising

6. According to the essay, all of the following are reasons that Michael Gove wants *Blackadder* banned from schools EXCEPT for:
   (A) *Blackadder* encourages left-wing myths
   (B) *Blackadder* portrays the First World War in a negative manner
   (C) *Blackadder* does not teach about the First World War in the "right way"
   (D) *Blackadder* is a medium of entertainment rather than education

7. The character of Captain Edmund Blackadder may best be described as
   (A) patriotic
   (B) self-sacrificing
   (C) naive
   (D) cynical

8. The word looming in paragraph 5 is closest in meaning to
   (A) becoming gloomy
   (B) about to happen
   (C) starting to retreat
   (D) appearing uncertain

9. [A], [B], [C] and [D] indicate where the following sentence can be added to paragraph 5. Mark your answer on your answer sheet.
   That is the question the British face in the debate over what it means to commemorate this war.

10. The essay implies that movies and television shows
    (A) quickly lose their social impact after a year or two.
    (B) are important primarily for their entertainment value.
    (C) can help stimulate discussions of important issues.
    (D) are appropriate for use in teaching foreign languages.

Summary

Read the sentences below and choose the statement that best summarises the main idea of paragraph 4.

(A) Rowan Atkinson became famous for his role in the television show, *Mr. Bean*.

(B) The main character in *Blackadder* is interested primarily in surviving the war.

(C) *Blackadder* graphically depicts the horrors of trench warfare on the Western Front.

Discussion

1. Do you feel the author provides an accurate account of the debate regarding Britain's role in World War I? Draw on your knowledge of films, current events or novels to support your view.

2. What are some issues that spark debate about other wars, such as World War II, Vietnam, or the Iraq War. Brainstorm and discuss what you know about these issues.

Homework / Research

Watch the movie *Oh! What a Lovely War* or some of the episodes of "Blackadder Goes Forth" (season four of *Blackadder*). Why do you think some people disapprove of or find these inappropriate? Be prepared to discuss what issues are involved. Do you think it is unpatriotic to criticise or protest your own country's involvement in a war? Be prepared to explain your view.

Chapter 8

Mod and Modern Britain

映画『さらば青春の光』(1979)より

Warming-Up Activities:

1. Brainstorming on the Topic

1960年代のイギリスらしい服装や音楽、ライフスタイルを挙げてみよう。それらのものは、日本、アジアの国々や世界の他の地域でも見られるだろうか？

2. Vocabulary

☐ emerge	自動 現れる	☐ consumerism	名 大量消費文化(cf. consumer)
☐ flourish	自動 繁盛する、栄える	☐ sophistication	名 洗練(形 sophisticated)
☐ celebrate	他動 〜を祝う(名 celebration)	☐ iconic	形 聖像の、(時代の)象徴的な(名 icon)
☐ integration	名 統合(他動 integrate)	☐ mythic	形 神話の、神話的な(名 myth)
☐ mobility	名 移動性、流動性(形 mobile)	☐ identity	名 アイデンティティ

Mod is short for modern. It's a set of ideas and attitudes, a style of dress and pop music that emerged in Britain in the late 1950s and flourished in the 1960s. Think of the Who and the Beatles, Mary Quant, Vespa scooters, narrow neckties, Italian suits and army-issue Parkas. A perennial influence on pop culture at home and abroad, Mod, as historian Richard Weight has recently argued, was not only Britain's equivalent of the American Dream; it was also "the first British youth culture to celebrate technology, art and design, cosmopolitanism, racial integration, sexual ambiguity and social mobility." It offered an optimism about the future—and that may be why as an expression of social freedom coupled with consumerism, it has been reinvented and exported while also remaining quintessentially British.

[A] Mod can be traced to the nightclubs of London's Soho district in the late 1950s and the fashionable youth who called themselves "Modernists" for their love of modern jazz. [B] They were working-class youth inspired by both American consumerism and European sophistication. [C] Across Britain the income of young people had increased by 50 percent since 1945—with recorded music accounting for more than 40 percent of their purchases. Fashion offered new identities. [D] But Mod soon left its working-class beginnings standing for all things new and British in the 1960s. Scholars debate the Mod narrative: Was it an authentic youth movement that was co-opted by commercialisation or were Mods crafting new identities out of consumption? Equally important is the "moral panic" it caused among the British public about youth culture and delinquency in the 1960s. A number of towns saw clashes between Mods and Rockers, a rival gang. Front-page news of vandalism and violence between gangs and police shocked Britons. On the Whitsun weekend of 1964, 1,000 youths rioted in Brighton.

The Mod-Rocker clashes are the backdrop for *Brighton Rock* (2010), a re-make of a 1947 film adapted from Graham Greene's 1938 novel. This iconic moment in 1960s Britain underscores the film's message. Pinkie Browne is a petty mobster who seeks revenge and power after the leader of his gang is murdered by rivals. A young waitress named Rose has knowledge of Pinkie's revenge killing, so Pinkie decides to court and marry her to ensure the truth does not get out, telling her "We're both old fashioned" and revealing his deep Catholicism. Later, Pinkie steals a scooter and dons an army jacket, passing himself off as a Mod to use the rioting as a <u>cover</u> for his violent plan. Rose, too, buys herself a Mod ensemble, but her action is a sign of hope that both can escape to new lives. But both are fated to be left behind. As Pinkie says near the end of the film, taking the stick candy sold on Brighton pier as analogy: "People don't change. It's like a stick of rock. Bite it all the way down and you still read Brighton."

Mod has continued its influence on Britain and the world. The 1979 film *Quadrophenia*, based on the 1972 rock-opera by the Who, is largely responsible for a Mod revival in the 1980s, led by the Jam, whose lead singer and guitarist Paul Weller was inspired by the English themes of the Kinks' Ray Davies. Britpop of the 1990s— including the bands Oasis, Blur, and Suede—drew on Mod to counter American music influence. Meanwhile, Mod movements have surfaced in the US and Japan, among others. *We Are the Mods* is an American film about the contemporary Mod scene in Los Angeles. A Mods Mayday scooter parade is an annual Tokyo event. Ironically, according to some, British Mod today has lost much of its former international outlook, becoming nationalistic and xenophobic. Whatever its current status, Mod remains, as Christine Feldman suggests, an almost mythic version of British youth identity and a continuing source of national pride.

映画『ブライトン・ロック』(2010)より

Notes

- l. 5: **equivalent** 名 等価のもの
- l. 7: **ambiguity** 名 曖昧さ
- l. 10: **quintessentially** 副 本質的に
- l. 23: **Whitsun** 聖霊降臨祭 (= Whitsunday 復活祭後の第7日曜日)
- l. 22: **vandalism** 名 破壊行為
- l. 24: **Brighton** ブライトン (イングランド南部の都市)
- l. 27: **underscores > underscore** 他動 〜を強調する
- l. 27: **mobster** 名 ギャングの一員
- l. 47: **xenophobic** 形 外国人嫌いの

Comprehension

1. In paragraph 1, the author suggests that
   (A) Mod culture is an important part of British culture.
   (B) Mod culture is the British counterpart of the American Dream.
   (C) Mod culture is an expression of class conflict in Britain.
   (D) Mod culture reached its height of popularity in the 1950s.

2. According to the passage, all of the ideas or items are part of Mod culture EXCEPT:
   (A) Italian fashions and pop music
   (B) racial harmony
   (C) criticism of the British class system
   (D) a positive outlook on modern life

3. The phrase a perennial influence in paragraph 1 is closest in meaning to
   (A) a recurring force
   (B) a beautiful flower
   (C) an annual event
   (D) a rare incident

4. Which of the following facts is NOT true according to the passage?
   (A) Postwar youth were less affluent than youth before them.
   (B) The first Mods took their name from the music they loved.
   (C) Mod originated in London in the 1950s.
   (D) Postwar British youth spent a considerable amount of their income on music.

5. The phrase standing for in paragraph 2 is closest in meaning to
   (A) putting up with
   (B) tolerating
   (C) getting up
   (D) referring to

6. The noun <u>cover</u> in paragraph 3 is closest in meaning to
   (A) protection
   (B) weapon
   (C) disguise
   (D) song

7. [A], [B], [C] and [D] indicate where the following sentence can be added to paragraph 2. Mark the answer on your answer sheet.
   For them, postwar consumer society seemed to offer a way out of the rigid class system.

8. Which of the following statements is NOT made in the passage?
   (A) The Jam drew influence from Ray Davies.
   (B) The contemporary US has its own Mod scene.
   (C) English towns were the sites of youth violence during the 1950s.
   (D) There has been a previous film adaptation of Greene's novel.

9. Which of the following claims is NOT made about Mod culture in the passage?
   (A) British Mod culture has changed since the 1960s.
   (B) Mod movements have surfaced in other countries.
   (C) Scholars are divided about the nature of the Mod movement in the 1960s.
   (D) Mod culture in Britain today has strongly cosmopolitan outlook.

10. Which claim about *Brighton Rock* is NOT true according to the passage?
    (A) Pinkie and Rose are doomed characters.
    (B) The Mod element of the film helps to highlight the message of the film.
    (C) An important theme of the film is conveyed through the Brighton Rock candy.
    (D) Pinkie courts Rose by convincing her that they need to start a new life.

Summary

Read the sentences below and choose the sentence that best summarises paragraph 2.

(A) The arrival of consumer society after World War II offered working class youth the possibility of increased social mobility.

(B) The Mod movement was an authentic grassroots youth culture that was commercialised by corporate interests.

(C) Modern jazz remained an important influence on the development of the mod style throughout the 1960s.

Discussion

Discuss the charging nature of Mod culture as outlined in the essay.

_____

Homework / Research

1. Explore the Mod Culture homepage and prepare to report on Mod movements around the world. <http://www.modculture.co.uk/>.

_____

2. Discuss the main differences between the recent *Brighton Rock* film and Graham Greene's 1938 novel. Do they help reveal the filmmaker's intent?

_____

3. In *"We Are the Mods": A Transnational History of a Youth Subculture*, Christine Jaqueline Feldman writes, "If Mod is tied to the contemporary as well as the mid-60s period, it is also connected to the futuristic visions promised by modernist design. More so than elsewhere, the digitally fast pace of Japanese cities and the mass of neon that illuminates them seem to fulfil this promise" (150). Assess this statement by researching Mod culture in Japan.

Chapter 9

"A green and pleasant land"?:
Social Order and the English Countryside

典型的なイングランドの田舎の風景

Warming-Up Activities:

1. Brainstorming on the Topic

イギリスの田舎について自分が持っているイメージを挙げてみよう。どんな人たちやイベント、どんなライフスタイルを思い浮かべるだろうか？

2. Vocabulary

☐ adapt	自動 (to ~に)順応する 他動 ~を(to...に)順応させる	☐ tension	名 緊張
☐ ideal	名 理想 形 理想的な	☐ medium	名 媒体
☐ rural	形 田舎の	☐ multicultural	形 多文化主義的な
☐ contest	他動 ~に異議を唱える	☐ estate	名 地所、屋敷
☐ stable	形 安定した (名 stability)	☐ upset	他動 ~を転覆する、狼狽させる

Reading

The image of England as a "green and pleasant land" derives from a poem by William Blake (1757-1827), written as the industrial revolution was reshaping the English social and economic order. Adapted as an inspirational hymn entitled "Jerusalem" at the height of class conflict, war and empire early in the twentieth century, the hymn aimed to inspire Britons to build an ideal social order, a new Jerusalem. Even today, it is the rural society of the manor and the village, a traditional community rooted in a stable hierarchical order, that remains an essential—although contested and much commodified—ideal.

In the 20th century, British pop music reflected the tensions of the new and the old. Indeed, as Britain celebrated all things modern—or Mod—in the 1960s, a band such as The Kinks, known for a string of rock and R & B hits, helped create a distinctive pop version of Englishness. Banned from entering the US at the height of their popularity, the group turned to English themes, most notably in the *Village Green Preservation Society* (1968). Songwriter Ray Davies tempered nostalgia with satire of English society. [A] The title track from the album, in which a collective "we" sings of "preserving the old ways from being abused", manages to be both ironic and sentimental. [B] Through the 1960s and 70s, British folk traditions informed music, especially Led Zeppelin, Fairport Convention and Jethro Tull. [C] Englishness persisted in Mod revival bands such as the Jam and in the new wave of XTC while Britpop artists such as Oasis, Blur and Pulp in the 1990s drew inspiration from Davies and the Beatles. [D]

Television has been an especially important medium for exploring tradition, modernity and the rural order, as demonstrated by the popularity of *Upstairs, Downstairs* (1971-75) and *Brideshead Revisited* (1981). Tourism is one spinoff industry of recent TV series while controversy has arisen around whether these images of Englishness suit a multicultural nation. Popular crime drama *Midsomer Murders* (1997-) offers loving depictions of the English countryside while entertaining with an ever-changing cast of eccentric "folk" embroiled in sex, intrigue and murder—an average of three murders per episode. Chief Inspector Tom Barnaby has a deep suspicion of the countryside and its vaunted traditions; however, his loving wife Joyce is an enthusiast for all things local. Fans of the show can follow the Midsomer Murders Trail, a tour of 130 murder scenes in the beautiful Buckinghamshire countryside. Thus, it's no wonder that the show's producer called the series "a bastion of Englishness" in 2011, only to ignite controversy when he went on to insist that the programme would not be successful with "ethnic minorities" in the "English village". *Downton Abbey* (2010-), a period drama set in a country estate at the beginning of the century, follows the lives of the aristocratic Crawley family and its retinue of servants. War, women's suffrage and class conflict swirl threateningly around the stable hierarchy of the country estate. The first season, which covers the years 1912 to 1914, opens with the sinking of the Titanic and the death of the heir to Downton, plunging the estate into crisis. Meanwhile, both class and ethnic others upset the balance: the eldest daughter Lady Mary has an affair with a Turkish diplomat, which threatens to ruin her marriage prospects, and distant cousin and middle-class lawyer Matthew Crawley and his mother struggle to adapt to aristocratic life.

TVドラマ『バーナビー警部』（1997～）より

Notes

- l. 2: **industrial revolution** 産業革命　● l. 3: **inspirational** 形 霊感を与える、感動させる　● l. 3: **hymn** 名 賛歌、賛美歌　● l. 4: **class conflict** 階級の対立　● l. 6: **manor** 封建領主の大邸宅　● l. 7: **hierarchical** 形 階層的な、上下関係が厳しい(hierarchy 名 階層)　● l. 8: **commodified > commodify** 他動 ～を商品化する　● l. 23: **spinoff** 名 スピンオフ、(人気番組などの)続編　● l. 27: **embroiled > embroil** 他動 ～を(in…に)巻き込む　● l. 27: **intrigue** 名 陰謀　● l. 30: **vaunted** 形 自慢の　● l. 34: **Buckinghamshire** バッキンガムシャー(イングランド南部の州)　● l. 36: **bastion** 名 要塞、砦　● l. 40: **retinue** 名 従者　● l. 41: **women's suffrage** 婦人参政権　● l. 41: **swirl** 自動 渦巻く　● l. 43: **the Titanic** タイタニック号(1912年に氷山と衝突して沈没した豪華客船)

Comprehension

1. In paragraph 1, the author claims that
   - (A) The industrial revolution helped develop English society.
   - (B) Rural England continues to offer an attractive social ideal.
   - (C) William Blake was an important influence on the new social order.
   - (D) Popular hymns reflected the changing social order.

2. Which of the facts about British music is NOT true?
   - (A) British folk music influenced popular music of the 1960s and 70s.
   - (B) Tensions between modern and traditional life were reflected in music.
   - (C) The Kinks included English themes in their music.
   - (D) Ray Davies offered a deeply sentimental view of English culture.

3. The phrase it's no wonder that in paragraph 3 is closest in meaning to
   - (A) it's amazing that
   - (B) it's not surprising that
   - (C) it's rather unexceptional that
   - (D) it's quite surprising that

4. Which of the following facts are NOT true according to the passage?
   - (A) "Jerusalem" was adapted to music during a period of social unrest.
   - (B) Oasis, Pulp and Blur featured English themes in their music.
   - (C) The Jam and XTC formed part of the mod revival in the late 1970s.
   - (D) *Upstairs, Downstairs* and *Brideshead Revisited* were popular dramas.

5. The phrase ignite controversy in paragraph 3 is closest in meaning to
   - (A) provoke condemnation
   - (B) inspire innovation
   - (C) show clearly
   - (D) criticise severely

6. The word plunging in paragraph 3 is closest in meaning to
   (A) diving in
   (B) damaging
   (C) forcing
   (D) finishing off

7. [A], [B], [C] and [D] indicate where the following sentence can be added to paragraph 2. Mark the answer on your answer sheet.
   Ironically, the youth counter culture of these decades seemed to embrace aspects of the traditional aristocratic life with rockstars such as Brian Jones, Mick Jagger and Jimmy Page acquiring manor estates in the countryside.

8. Which theme is NOT discussed in the passage?
   (A) tradition
   (B) modern life
   (C) music in television drama
   (D) ethnic minorities

9. Which of the following claims is NOT made in the essay?
   (A) The Kinks celebrated English culture in their music.
   (B) *Downton Abbey* dramatises class conflict.
   (C) "The Village Green Preservation Society" voices concerns about maintaining English traditions.
   (D) Recent depictions of the countryside show it as a place of virtue and order.

10. Which fact about the television dramas is true according to the passage?
    (A) The producer of *Midsomer Murders* preferred plots involving white Britons.
    (B) Matthew Crawley of *Downton Abbey* represents middle class virtue and hard work.
    (C) The lead characters of *Midsomer Murders* dislike the people and traditions of the countryside.
    (D) Lady Mary is continually challenging the authority of Robert Grantham, the Lord of Downton Abbey.

Summary

Read the sentences below and choose the sentence that best summarises paragraph 3.

(A) Television has helped correct the idealised view of the English countryside.

(B) Social change in rural England continues to be the subject of interest in television series.

(C) Television programmes have for the most part offered controversial depictions of English life.

Discussion

1. What evidence does the author offer to support the claim that British pop music has reflected the tensions of the traditional and the modern? Can you think of English pop songs that are not fundamentally nostalgic?

2. In your opinion, how should a concept such as Englishness be defined? Should it reflect founding ethnic groups and traditional culture or should it keep pace with demographic and cultural changes?

Homework / Research

1. Watch further episodes of *Midsomer Murders*. What typically English cultural themes does the programme feature? What are the characters' attitudes toward these examples of Englishness? What do you think is the appeal of the series outside the UK (in Japan, for example, where it is currently broadcast)?

2. Watch episodes of season 1 and beyond of *Downton Abbey*. What importance does the question of marriage and inheritance play in the drama? What other themes are developed? Do you agree that the series attempts to depict an ideal English social order? Explain.

Chapter 10

Monty Python's *Life of Brian*:
Comedy or Blasphemy?

映画『ライフ・オブ・ブライアン』(1979)より

Warming-Up Activities:

1. Brainstorming on the Topic

どんな話題でもお笑い番組やコメディの題材にしてもいいのだろうか？　それとも、笑いのネタにしてはいけない話題があるのだろうか？　意見を述べてみよう。

2. Vocabulary

- ☐ blasphemy　　名 冒瀆 (形 blasphemous)
- ☐ disgust　　名 嫌悪感　他動 ～をむかつかせる
- ☐ preach　　自動 説教する、神の教えを説く
- ☐ execution　　名 処刑、実行 (他動 execute)
- ☐ condemn　　他動 ～を非難する
- ☐ allusion　　名 言及 (自動 allude)
- ☐ gospel　　名 福音書
- ☐ sacrilegious　　形 冒瀆的な (名 sacrilege)
- ☐ evoke　　他動 ～を引き起こす、喚起する
- ☐ hypocrisy　　名 偽善

Reading

When the British comedy group Monty Python released *Life of Brian* in 1979, they were at their creative and performing peak. They had already made a name for themselves with their innovative BBC television series, *Monty Python's Flying Circus* (1969-1974) and had also released in 1975 the film *Monty Python and the Holy Grail*, fast on its way to becoming a cult classic. In *Holy Grail*, the Pythons (as they are known to fans) had trained their comedic talent on the historical figure of King Arthur. With *Life of Brian*, however, they raised the stakes and focused on life in Judea at the time of Jesus Christ.

映画『ライフ・オブ・ブライアン』(1979)より

The Python members knew their film would invite controversy, but they were unprepared for the level of anger and disgust that it engendered. *Life of Brian* was attacked by various religious groups as "sinful", "profane" and "blasphemous". All six members of Monty Python received death threats. In England the film was banned outright in many localities or limited to those over eighteen years old.

[A] Ironically, for a movie that caused such a backlash from the religious community, the character of Jesus has, at best, a brief "cameo" role preaching the Sermon on the Mount. [B] The title character and central figure is Brian Cohen—born the same night as Jesus but in the manger next door. [C] Brian grows up and, through bizarre chance alone, becomes an unwilling messianic figure, despite his repeatedly insisting, "I am not the Messiah!" Paradoxically, Brian's sole commandment is: "Don't let anyone tell you what to do." [D]

Believers found three scenes particularly objectionable. First, early in the movie, Jesus preaches the "The Sermon on the Mount" to a gathering of people. The unruly crowd, however, mishears "blessed are the peace makers" as "blessed are the cheese makers." Second, midway through the movie, Brian is arrested by the Romans and sentenced to be crucified. As the prisoners are being led to the execution site, a man steps out of the crowd to take a condemned man's cross and carry it for him—an allusion to the gospel account of Simon of Cyrene's carrying Christ's cross. However, the man immediately scurries off, leaving the Simon-stand-in to be crucified in his stead. Finally, the scene most often criticised is the final one where Brian is crucified on a hilltop along with dozens of other "criminals". As Brian looks off in despair, the man to his right advises him to "cheer up" and then breaks into singing "Always Look on the Bright Side of Life" with the other crucified men whistling in accompaniment.

Upon closer examination, though, the accusation of "sacrilegious mockery" is suspect. In the Sermon on the Mount scene, the joke is on the crowd bickering over the interpretation of "cheese makers," not on Jesus. Regarding the "Simon-with-the-cross" scene, there is no indication that the man who runs away is intended to be Jesus, as many viewers mistakenly believe. Last, Jesus is not among those crucified at the end. However, given the power of the cross as a Christian icon, it is not surprising that the hilltop crucifixion scene would evoke a strong negative response from some quarters.

Finally, one indication of the cultural significance of *Life of Brian* is that in 2011, BBC4 aired the comedy drama, *Holy Flying Circus,* a recreation of the making of *Life of Brian* and the ensuing controversy. Clearly, *Life of Brian* remains not only a comedy classic and potent criticism of all manner of hypocrisy, but a cultural milestone as well. Though, as Brian might say, "See it for yourself and decide."

Notes

- l. 4 : **the Holy Grail** 聖杯（イエス・キリストが最後の晩餐で用い、十字架にかけられた際に血の受け皿として使われたという杯）
- l. 6 : **King Arthur** アーサー王（6世紀頃の伝説のイギリス王）
- l. 7 : **Judea** ユダヤ（古代パレスチナの南部地域で、現代のユダヤ人は Jewish, Jew などと表現する）
- l. 11 : **engendered > engender** 他動 〜を生み出す
- l. 16 : **localities > locality** 名 付近、場所
- l. 18 : **cameo** 名 カメオ、一場面だけの出演
- l. 18-19 : **the Sermon on the Mount** 山上の教訓（イエスが山の上で弟子と群衆に語った重要な教え、またはその場面）
- l. 21 : **messianic** 形 救世主の
- l. 22 : **commandment** 名 命令、掟（モーセの「十戒」を Ten Commandments と言う）
- l. 24 : **objectionable** 形 反対すべき、異議のある
- l. 36 : **mockery** 名 嘲り、からかい
- l. 37 : **bickering > bicker** 自動 言い争う
- l. 45 : **ensuing > ensue** 自動 続いて起こる
- l. 46 : **potent** 形 力強い、有力な
- l. 46 : **all manner of** あらゆる

Comprehension

1. According to the essay, all of the following are true about *Life of Brian* EXCEPT for:
   (A) The Monty Python group was unprepared to make the movie.
   (B) *Life of Brian* was made after *Holy Grail*.
   (C) In some places the movie was not allowed to be shown.
   (D) The movie was then probably Monty Python's most ambitious work.

2. According to the essay, who is Simon of Cyrene?
   (A) One member of the Monty Python group.
   (B) A character in the Bible.
   (C) The Messiah.
   (D) A BBC television producer.

3. The expression made a name for themselves in paragraph 1 is closest in meaning to
   (A) chosen names for their characters
   (B) decided to call themselves "Monty Python"
   (C) worked with well-known people
   (D) become famous and respected

4. The word outright in paragraph 2 is closest in meaning to
   (A) finally
   (B) completely
   (C) sometimes
   (D) right now

5. According to the essay, what do Brian and Jesus have in common?
   (A) They were born in the same room.
   (B) They were born on the same day.
   (C) They have the same parents.
   (D) They are both the Messiah.

6. The part of Jesus in *Life of Brian* may best be described as
   - (A) controversial.
   - (B) sacrilegious.
   - (C) central.
   - (D) minor.

7. The expression <u>scurries off</u> in paragraph 4 is closest in meaning to
   - (A) hides quickly.
   - (B) walks away quietly.
   - (C) jumps down.
   - (D) hurries away.

8. The expression <u>some quarters</u> in paragraph 5 most likely refers to
   - (A) Monty Python fans
   - (B) Christian believers
   - (C) the "criminals" who were crucified
   - (D) members of Monty Python

9. [A], [B], [C] and [D] indicate where the following sentence can be added to paragraph 3. Mark your answer on your answer sheet.
   Still, the religious outcry resulted from the belief that the Pythons had made a sacrilegious mockery of the life and death of Christ.

10. The author cites the film *Holy Flying Circus* as an example of
    - (A) a sacrilegious movie.
    - (B) the importance of *Life of Brian*.
    - (C) a comedy classic.
    - (D) an early Monty Python movie.

Summary

Read the sentences below and choose the statement that best summarises the main idea of paragraph 6.

(A) The accusations of "sacrilegious mockery" need closer examination.

(B) The accusations of "sacrilegious mockery" are justified but surprising.

(C) The accusations of "sacrilegious mockery" are unjustified, but not surprising.

Discussion

1. Do you feel the author provides an accurate account of the debate regarding how far comedy should go? Are subjects such as religious figures off limits? Draw on your knowledge of films, current events or novels to support your view.

2. Do you know of any movies in Japan that some people wanted banned for religious or other reasons? If so, what were their reasons? How did you feel?

Homework / Research

1. Watch *Life of Brian* and be prepared to discuss what you think caused some religious groups to respond so negatively to the film. Pay special attention to the scenes mentioned in the essay.

2. Watch *Holy Flying Circus* and be prepared to summarise and present what you learned about the making of *Life of Brian* and the resulting controversy.

Chapter 11

Sherlock:
A Holmes for Our Time

TVドラマ『シャーロック』(2010〜)より

Warming-Up Activities:

1. Brainstorming on the Topic

サー・アーサー・コナン・ドイル(Sir Arthur Conan Doyle) とシャーロック・ホームズについてどんなことを知っているだろう？ ホームズ物の短編小説や長編小説を読んだことがあるだろうか？ シャーロック・ホームズの登場する映画はどうだろう？ もしその経験があるなら、それらの作品の感想は？

2. Vocabulary

☐ recognise	他動 〜を認識する	☐ definitive	形 決定的な、決定版の
☐ evolution	名 進化 (自動 evolve)	☐ psychological	形 心理的な、心理学的な
☐ acknowledge	他動 〜を認める	☐ portrayal	他動 描写、演技による再現
☐ faithful	形 忠実な	☐ affiliation	名 提携、所属
☐ update	他動 〜を最新のものにする、〜に最新情報を提供する	☐ ubiquitous	形 どこにでも現れる、偏在する

Reading

The character of Sherlock Holmes first appeared in print in 1887 in the novel *A Study in Scarlet* by Sir Arthur Conan Doyle. Sherlock Holmes would go on to become one of the most popular and recognised fictional characters as the hero in fifty-six short stories and four novels. The development of motion-picture technology in the late 19th century opened the door to an extension of this popularity well beyond the world of books and magazines. The evolution of Sherlock Holmes as a film phenomenon progressed almost in tandem with the development of film itself as a narrative medium.

Holmes makes his film debut in a thirty-five second silent parody, *Sherlock Holmes Baffled*, in 1900, and appears in 1905 in the first Holmes-inspired properly narrative film, *Adventures of Sherlock Holmes.* From then on into the 20th century and beyond it is a virtual flood of Sherlock Holmes material on to film and, later, television. The *Guinness World Records*, for example, acknowledges Sherlock Holmes as the "most portrayed movie character"—with more than seventy actors playing the part over the course of two hundred plus movies.

One of the notable actors who have played Holmes is Basil Rathbone who, along with Nigel Bruce as Holmes' faithful sidekick, Dr John Watson, starred in a series of fourteen Sherlock Holmes films (1939-1946). The films created a controversy when the story was updated to the 1940s. For some fans, the idea of Sherlock Holmes hunting down Nazis is sacrilegious. For others, though, modernisation opens up unlimited creative possibilities and saves Conan Doyle's stories from becoming over-stuffed Victorian museum pieces. For many, Jeremy Brett remains the definitive Holmes. Brett, with David Burke and later Edward Hardwicke as Watson, played Holmes in forty-one episodes of *Sherlock Holmes* for Britain's Granada Television (1984-1994). Known for plumbing the psychological depths of the character for his "warts and all" portrayal of Sherlock Holmes, Brett has become a steadfast and beloved icon of British pop culture.

It seems that each generation needs a Sherlock Holmes of its own. BBC's recent television series, *Sherlock* (with Benedict Cumberbatch as Holmes and Martin Freeman as Watson), makes no bones about its contemporary affiliations. [A] From its premier episode's (July, 2010) opening directly with hand-held video footage of soldiers in Afghanistan to the ubiquitous presence of smart phones, laptops, and other high-tech hardware, *Sherlock* announces: this is a 21st-century Sherlock Holmes. [B] At the heart of the series is the relationship between Holmes and Watson. [C] As Alan Barnes notes in *Sherlock Holmes on Screen*, what is most revolutionary about *Sherlock* is that it is never Holmes and Watson but always "Sherlock and John". [D] *Sherlock* is as much about trust and friendship as it is about solving crimes.

Finally, it may be the relationship between the show's fandom and the creators and writers of *Sherlock* (Steven Moffat and Mark Gatiss) that make this series stand out from other Sherlock Holmes productions. Moffat and Gatiss mention in an interview that they acknowledge and pay attention to the creativity and dedication of their passionate fans. For example, at the end of the second series Sherlock appears to have jumped to his death. Immediately, using the hashtag "#sherlocklives", social network sites lit up with theories of how Sherlock may have faked his death. In the opening episode of the third series, when a text message sent to a character's phone announces that Sherlock is indeed alive, "#sherlocklives" appears all over the television screen. As one young fan put it, "I felt like I was getting a huge hug from Moffat and Gatiss." Sir Arthur Conan Doyle would be pleased to know that the game is most certainly still afoot.

映画『シャーロック・ホームズ』(2009)より

Notes

- l. 11-12: **Guinness World Records** ギネス世界記録(アイルランドのビールメーカー Guinness PLC が作成するありとあらゆる分野の世界記録を綴ったもの)
- l. 20: **over-stuffed** 形 過度に詰め込まれた
- l. 24: **plumbing > plumb** 他動 〜を測り知る
- l. 25: **steadfast** 形 忠実な、しっかりした
- l. 29: **footage** 名 映画のフィート数、録画された場面
- l. 37: **fandom** 名 すべてのファン、ファンの集合体
- l. 44: **hashtag** 名 ハッシュタグ (ツイッターなど SNS で主に使われる、#で始まってスペースのない文字列で作られたメタデータ・タグ)
- l. 46: **text message** 携帯電話のメール

Comprehension

1. According to the essay, what is the relation between movies and Sherlock Holmes?
   (A) Movies helped to increase the popularity of Sherlock Holmes.
   (B) People preferred to watch the movies instead of reading the stories.
   (C) In addition to the stories and novels, Doyle also wrote the screenplays.
   (D) Without the character of Sherlock Holmes, movies would not have survived.

2. The essay implies that *Sherlock Holmes Baffled* is most likely important
   (A) as the movie that made Sherlock Holmes famous.
   (B) as the first adaptation of a novel by Arthur Conan Doyle.
   (C) as a piece of movie history trivia.
   (D) as the first actual narrative movie.

3. The expression in tandem in paragraph 1 is closest in meaning to
   (A) unrelated
   (B) together
   (C) by chance
   (D) in competition

4. The author cites the *Guinness World Records* as
   (A) an example of a popular television series.
   (B) support for the claim of Sherlock Holmes' popularity.
   (C) a book about the history of Sherlock Holmes on film.
   (D) criticism of most actors who play Sherlock Holmes.

5. The word sidekick in paragraph 3 is closest in meaning to
   (A) servant
   (B) enemy
   (C) friend
   (D) assistant

6. Why were the Sherlock Holmes films starring Basil Rathbone controversial?
    (A) Basil Rathbone was not a British actor.
    (B) People thought Rathbone was too old to play Holmes.
    (C) The setting for the movies was not the Victorian era.
    (D) The movies were filmed in colour for the first time.

7. Jeremy Brett's portrayal of Sherlock Holmes is the favourite of many viewers because
    (A) he deeply understood the character of Sherlock Holmes.
    (B) he was a well-loved icon of British pop culture.
    (C) he was able to portray the best aspects of Sherlock Holmes.
    (D) he had a "warts and all" attitude about himself.

8. What does the essay imply is different about the current BBC *Sherlock* series?
    (A) The relation between Holmes and Watson is more personal and human.
    (B) *Sherlock* is very consciously set in the 21st century.
    (C) Fans of the series are directly involved in some of its creation.
    (D) A, B and C.

9. [A], [B], [C] and [D] indicate where the following sentence can be added to paragraph 4. Mark your answer on your answer sheet.
    ***Sherlock*, however, is more than just a slicker, sexier adaptation of the Sherlock Holmes canon.**

10. What does the essay imply about fans of *Sherlock*?
    (A) They spend too many hours a day commenting on social network sites.
    (B) Many believed that Sherlock had died at the end of the second series.
    (C) Some fans are disappointed that the series doesn't follow the stories closely.
    (D) They feel connected to the series because their opinions are taken into account.

Summary

Read the sentences below and choose the statement that best summarises the main idea of paragraph 3.

(A) The portrayals of Sherlock Holmes by Basil Rathbone and Jeremy Brett are both notable, but for different reasons.

(B) Of the portrayals of Sherlock Holmes by Basil Rathbone and Jeremy Brett, Brett's is clearly the superior performance.

(C) Without periodic modernisation, Sherlock Holmes movies would simply become quaint depictions of Victorian culture.

Discussion

1. Do you feel the author provides an accurate account of the debate regarding different film adaptations of the Sherlock Holmes stories. Draw on your knowledge of films, current events or novels to support your view.

2. Why do you think Sherlock Holmes continues to be such a popular fictional character? The essay states that over 200 Sherlock-related films have been made. What do you think makes the Sherlock Holmes material so attractive for film adaptation? What do you think the author means by, "It seems that each generation needs a Sherlock Holmes of its own"? Do you agree?

Homework / Research

Watch some earlier Sherlock Holmes films with actors such as Peter Cushing, Basil Rathbone, and Jeremy Brett. Compare how the adaptation of the material or the portrayal of Sherlock Holmes differs among the films. Watch some of the recent BBC *Sherlock* series and make note of the various ways in which this is a uniquely 21st-century Sherlock Holmes adaptation.

Chapter 12

"Century of Strangers":
Immigrants from Former British Colonies

ロンドンのイースト・エンドにあるブリックレーン（英語の下はベンガル語）

Warming-Up Activities:

1. Brainstorming on the Topic

エスニック・マイノリティ(ethnic minorities)はイギリスの全人口の8%を占め、ロンドンなど都市部ではもっと大きな比率となる。イギリスのエスニック・マイノリティについて知っている人物やキーワードを英語で書き出してみよう。

2. Vocabulary

- ☐ immigrant　　名 移民(行動は immigration)
- ☐ migrate　　　自動 移住する(名 migration)
- ☐ colony　　　　名 植民地
- ☐ reconstruct　　他動 〜を立て直す
- ☐ nationality　　名 国籍(cf. citizenship)
- ☐ promote　　　他動 〜を促進する(名 promotion)
- ☐ diversity　　　名 多様性(形 diverse)
- ☐ aggravate　　　他動 〜を悪化させる
- ☐ legislation　　名 立法、法律
- ☐ analyse　　　　他動 〜を分析する

Reading

"This has been the century of strangers, brown, yellow and white," says the narrator of Zadie Smith's critically acclaimed first novel, *White Teeth* (2000), "This has been the century of the great immigrant experiment." After World War II, so many people migrated from former UK colonies such as India and Jamaica to Britain, which needed a cheap workforce to reconstruct its economy, that, like a chemical "experiment", this mass migration has reshaped Britain's cultural landscape. An uninformed tourist might think Britain is a "white" nation and therefore that many non-white workers in the service sector are "foreigners". He or she would be surprised to know they are British. "Really? I didn't know they're British. They look different." This may sound naïve, but it points to the most hotly debated issue in Britain: the integration of immigrants. They *are* British by nationality, but unfortunately, increasingly many people find it a problem.

The 1990s and the early 2000s were marked by the increasing visibility of "Black British", British citizens of Asian and Afro-Caribbean descents. People celebrated "difference", as if to prove Britain's successful implementation of multiculturalism, a set of policies to promote cultural diversity. [A] *Goodness Gracious Me* (1996-98), a radio comedy written and played by British Asian actors and actresses, won great popularity and later became a TV programme (1998-2001). In one sketch, drunken Indians abuse an English waiter. In the past, English hooligans used to abuse Indian waiters in reality. [B] On the contrary, they loved it. In 1996, Meera Syal, an actress from *Goodness Gracious Me*, wrote an autobiographical novel *Anita and Me*, which was adapted for film in 2002. It nostalgically retells a British Indian girl Meena's friendship with a white working-class girl Anita. [C] The film adds a twist to the novel. Towards the end, Meena remembers Anita's greeting card, which shows her effort to respect what is important for her friend's family: "Then at Christmas, I got a card from Anita—a fat Santa

ロンドン中心部の様子

saying 'Merry Christmas'; she'd crossed out the Christmas bit and written 'Merry Divali', spelt wrong, of course, and a curly signature with three kisses underneath." [D]

However, multiculturalism in Britain has been seriously questioned since "7/7", or the London terrorist bombings that took place on 7 July 2005. As the four alleged suicide bombers were British Muslims descended from immigrants (Pakistani and Jamaican), Britons have begun to talk about the "failure" of multiculturalism more vocally. They want "cohesion", not "difference". They criticise the government for aggravating the radicalisation of British Muslims by promoting the superficial "cult of difference". However, it is a moot point whether Britain's multiculturalism is the only reason for their radicalisation. *Britz* (2007), for example, suggests they might have also been radicalised by the government's anti-terror legislation that has been tightened since the multiple terror attacks in the US on 11 September 2001— commonly known as "9/11". The drama centres on British Muslims, who are alienated by a new anti-terrorism act which they think only targets them. The hero works for MI5, often crushed by the thought that he is being used by the white establishment solely to investigate his own family and friends. His sister eventually chooses to be a suicide bomber. This drama has divided its viewers. Some criticise it for being too sympathetic with radicalised British Muslims, while others claim this is just white men's fantasy (as the drama was written and directed by a white Englishman). Still others consider it as a brave attempt to analyse this new "condition of England" question from a new perspective. This "great immigrant experiment" is not over yet, nor does anyone know whether it is a success.

Notes

- l. 2 : **acclaimed** 形 賞賛されている ● l. 5 : **workforce** 名 労働力 ● l. 8 : **service sector** サービス業（一般的に「業界」は industry） ● l. 14 : **multiculturalism** 名 多文化主義（内容については本文参照）
- l. 18 : **hooligan** 名 ごろつき、フーリガン（サッカー・チームの応援を口実に迷惑行為や暴力行為におよぶ人々）
- l. 18 : **abuse** 他動 〜の悪口を言う、〜を虐待する ● l. 28 : **Divali** 名 ヒンドゥー教の祭り Diwali のこと
- l. 31 : **alleged** 形 〜とされている（e.g. an alleged murderer 殺人犯と疑われている人） ● l. 35 : **radicalisation** 名 過激化、急進化 > **radical** 形 過激な、急進的な ● l. 36 : **moot point** 議論の余地がある点 ● l. 41 : **MI5 = Military Intelligence Section 5** 名 イギリス諜報部第5部（国内とイギリス連邦内の担当）

Comprehension

1. In paragraph 1, the author suggests
   (A) after World War II, Britain sought those who would work at low wages.
   (B) every tourist is confused about ethnic minorities in Britain.
   (C) politicians pay little attention to the integration of immigrants.
   (D) ethnic minorities in the UK should not be given British citizenship.

2. By this mass migration has reshaped Britain's cultural landscape, the author means
   (A) British landscape paintings have developed because many people left Britain.
   (B) the outlook of British cities has changed because many people left Britain.
   (C) the characteristics of British culture have changed because many people came to settle in to Britain.
   (D) the British countryside has been industrialised because many people came to settle in to Britain.

3. The word naïve in paragraph 1 is closest in meaning to
   (A) sensitive
   (B) tough
   (C) helpful
   (D) innocent

4. The increasing visibility of "Black British" is best illustrated by the fact that
   (A) more and more "Black British" people have had a future vision.
   (B) more and more "Black British" people have appeared in the media.
   (C) "Black British" people have become more and more forward-thinking.
   (D) "Black British" people have become more and more radicalised.

5. The word implementation in paragraph 2 is closest in meaning to
   (A) astonishment
   (B) execution
   (C) generalisation
   (D) threat

6. The following facts can be inferred from the phrase <u>of course</u> in paragraph 2 EXCEPT
   (A) Anita does not know much about traditional Indian customs.
   (B) Anita often misspells words.
   (C) "Diwali" is a difficult word for white English people.
   (D) "Diwali" is tiresome for white English people.

7. [A], [B], [C] and [D] indicate where the following sentence can be added to paragraph 2. Mark the answer on your answer sheet.
   This reversal of roles did not offend young white English viewers.

8. By <u>multiculturalism in Britain has been seriously questioned</u>, the author means
   (A) people have begun to answer questions about multiculturalism in Britain.
   (B) people have begun to ask questions about multiculturalism in Britain.
   (C) people have begun to doubt multiculturalism in Britain is a failure.
   (D) people have begun to suspect multiculturalism in Britain is a failure.

9. The word <u>cohesion</u> in paragraph 3 is closest in meaning to
   (A) openness
   (B) success
   (C) unity
   (D) wealth

10. According to paragraph 3, all of the following statements are true EXCEPT:
    (A) It was not until the London bombers were arrested that British people started to criticise the government's promotion of multiculturalism.
    (B) Some British people suspect the government have allowed British Muslims to be more extremist and more militant.
    (C) In *Britz*, British Muslims find the government's anti-terror legislation unfair.
    (D) The viewers of *Britz* are split in their view of the drama.

Summary

Read the sentences below and choose the statement that best summarises paragraph 2.

(A) In the 1990s and the early 2000s, more people immigrated to Britain than any other decade in history.

(B) In the 1990s and the early 2000s, people of immigrant origins enjoyed great success, leaving white people behind.

(C) In the 1990s and the early 2000s, British people appreciated new voices from people of immigrant origins.

Discussion

1. How would you compare the essay with recent films, novels, newspaper articles or webpages concerning ethnic minorities in Britain? Do they provide similar pictures or very different pictures?

2. Do you think those films or novels reflect the reality of ethnic minorities in Britain? If so, to what extent?

Homework / Research

Find out more on ethnic minorities in Britain. Read articles on such figures as Enoch Powell, Stephen Lawrence, Salman Rushdie and Samina Malik, or key phrases such as "immigration cap" and "racial stereotypes" (or "ethnic stereotypes"). Watch films such as *East Is East* (1999; British Pakistani), *Bend It Like Beckham* (2002; British Indian), *Ae Fond Kiss* (2004; British Pakistani), *Kidulthood* (2006; British Afro-Caribbean), *Brick Lane* (2007; British Bangladeshi) and *Small Island* (2009; British Afro-Caribbean). Prepare to discuss the ways British Asians are represented in the media.

Chapter 13

The UK:
A Surveillance Society

映画『クローズド・サーキット』(2013)より

ロンドンのCCTV(防犯カメラ)

Warming-Up Activities:

1. Brainstorming on the Topic

公共の場に設置された防犯カメラを見てどう感じるだろう？ 安全だと思うだろうか？ インターネット上でのプライバシーについてどんなことを知っているだろう？ インターネットやメール、携帯電話を使うことでプライバシーが侵される危険があることを知っているだろうか？

2. Vocabulary

☐ surveillance	名 監視	☐ pry	自動 (into 〜を)詮索する
☐ monitor	他動 〜を監視する、傍受する	☐ expose	他動 〜を(to…に)さらす、暴露する
☐ prompt	他動 〜を駆り立てる、促す	☐ tyrant	名 専制君主、独裁者(cf. tyranny)
☐ revelation	名 暴露、啓示(他動 reveal)	☐ obsess	他動 (通例 be obsessed with 〜に)取り憑かれる
☐ counterpart	名 よく似たもの、対応するもの	☐ assign	他動 〜を(to/for/as…に)任命する

Reading

The UK has more video surveillance cameras than any other nation on Earth. A 2006 report by an independent group of scholars counted more than 4 million CCTV (closed-circuit television) cameras in operation in the UK, or 1 camera for every 14 people. Dataveillance—the collection of information via mobile phones, credit cards and customer loyalty programmes (or point cards)—is also extremely high in Britain. In 2009, the Interception of Communications Commissioner (ICC) reported that the monitoring of phone calls, email and Internet activity had more than tripled since 1998. The "data-mining" of UK Internet users prompted the World Wide Web Foundation in a 2013 report to condemn the UK for failing to promote a "free and open" Internet, dropping the UK's ranking below a number of less-than-democratic states. How did Great Britain come to be such a model of surveillance society?

An answer to this question came from across the Atlantic in 2013, on revelations of extensive government surveillance of US and UK citizens alleged by former CIA contractor Edward Snowden. American observers noted that Britons were much less upset than their American counterparts. That's because Britons, the Americans claimed, trade freedom for social stability, believing that surveillance reduces crime. The British acceptance of surveillance, moreover, is rooted in its top-down power structure and a sheepish deference towards one's betters. For their part, UK commentators suggested that Hollywood films have for a long time naturalised various forms of surveillance in our everyday lives.

The latter point should go without saying: The cinema itself is part and parcel of our modern surveillance society. After all, aren't all movie-goers consummate voyeurs, prying into the private lives of the men and women depicted on screen? One notable—or notorious—British film on this theme is *Peeping Tom* (1960), directed by Michael Powell, which features a serial killer who uses a movie camera to record the deaths of his victims. The film was so controversial, the UK public so revolted by the topic that Powell, a major director at the time, had his career virtually destroyed. On one level, the film is about a sadistic killer who uses the camera to feed his violent fantasies. Yet on another level, it exposes the desire to see, to pry into the lives of others that is created in all visual media and is central to modern surveillance society.

Few contemporary films dare to be as troubling about surveillance society as Powell's, now considered a masterpiece. In part, we have reality TV to thank for a growing acceptance of surveillance in our lives. Popular programmes such as *Big Brother*, titled after George Orwell's dystopian tyrant, offer us the pleasure of watching others. Likewise, many contemporary British films employ the themes and technologies of surveillance as suspenseful entertainment. *Red Road* is a Scottish film about a CCTV operator in Glasgow who becomes obsessed with a man from her past, stalking him with her cameras, sometimes neglecting her duty to ensure public safety. The message is clear: Surveillance technology is neutral; it is humans who misuse it to violate our rights or cause us harm. *Closed Circuit* is a thriller that explores surveillance in the context of a terrorist attack. Martin Rose and Claudia Simmons Howe are barristers assigned to the Borough Market bombing, who soon learn that the case involves an MI5 cover-up of a failed operation against homegrown terrorists. The fact of surveillance is reiterated throughout the film—mostly on a stylistic level, with framing and establishing shots seen through single, sometimes multiple CCTV screens. These lend suspense to the plot, but the film shows surveillance as a force against which we are powerless. Not only our right to privacy but even our democratic rights, as seen in the miscarriage of justice that unfolds in the film, cannot be protected in the surveillance society.

Notes

- l. 6：**the Interception of Communications Commissioner** 通信傍受委員 ● l. 8：**the World Wide Web Foundation** WWWの維持と向上を目的とする国際機関 ● l. 17：**sheepish** 形 弱腰の ● l. 17：**deference** 名 服従 ● l. 21：**consummate** 形 完全な ● l. 21：**voyeur** 名 のぞき魔、詮索好きな人 ● l. 25：**revolted > revolt** 他動 ～をむかつかせる、～に反感を抱かせる ● l. 33：**dystopian** 形 ディストピア的な（dystopiaとは、utopiaの逆で、不幸や悪で満ちた世界のこと）● l. 36：**Glasgow** グラスゴー（スコットランドの工業都市）● l. 41：**Borough Market** バラ・マーケット（ロンドンのSouthwark地区にあるマーケット）● l. 41：**MI5** ＝第12章注釈参照 ● l. 42：**reiterated > reiterate** 他動 ～を反復する ● l. 43：**framing and establishing shots** エスタブリッシング・ショット（映画で、シーンの冒頭などで場所全体を撮るショット）

Comprehension

1. Which of the claims below is NOT made about films or TV programmes that deal with surveillance?
   (A) Reality TV programmes have made us more aware of the dangers of surveillance society.
   (B) With few exceptions, UK films have not challenged state surveillance on citizens.
   (C) Like US films, UK films dealing with surveillance tend to focus on the misuse of surveillance.
   (D) Surveillance themes and hi-tech increase the entertainment value of films.

2. Which of the facts below is NOT true of surveillance in the UK, according to the passage?
   (A) The UK has more surveillance cameras than any other nation in the world.
   (B) The ICC monitors and regulates "data-mining" in the UK.
   (C) The monitoring of private communications has risen three-fold since the late 1990s.
   (D) Some have questioned the UK's reputation for maintaining a "free and open" Internet.

3. Which of the claims below is true of the debate which followed the Snowden affair?
   (A) UK pundits blamed British television reality shows such as *Big Brother* for stirring up paranoia.
   (B) American commentators believe that Britons are more complacent about surveillance.
   (C) American commentators felt that there was an over-reaction about government spying.
   (D) UK commentators charged that US citizens care little about government surveillance.

4. The term data-mining in paragraph 1 refers to
   (A) the transmission of private communications and transactions
   (B) the destruction of private communications and transactions
   (C) the eavesdropping on private communications, shopping and web surfing
   (D) the monitoring of email communications

5. The verb phrase is rooted in in paragraph 2 is closest in meaning to
    (A) originates in (B) spread by
    (C) buried in (D) separate from

6. According to the passage, which of the statements below is NOT true of the film *Closed Circuit*?
    (A) The film is a thriller about the aftermath of a terrorist attack.
    (B) The film explores ways in which surveillance society can be resisted by citizens.
    (C) The lawyers on the case discover British intelligence is suppressing vital information.
    (D) The film uses CCTV shots to heighten suspense.

7. The phrase virtually destroyed in paragraph 3 is closest in meaning to
    (A) appearing to be broken (B) hardly damaged
    (C) almost ruined (D) untouched

8. The phrase lending suspense in paragraph 4 is closest in meaning to
    (A) reducing viewers' tension and anticipation
    (B) increasing viewers' tension and anticipation
    (C) creating surprise
    (D) provoking interest

9. Which of the following claims is NOT made regarding the film *Peeping Tom*?
    (A) The film probes the motivations for spying on others.
    (B) The film is a revolting and sensational treatment of murder.
    (C) The film is about a sick individual and his violent fantasies.
    (D) The film can be understood on at least two levels.

10. Which of the following facts is NOT true, according to the passage?
    (A) Powell's film has been rehabilitated among contemporary viewers.
    (B) The UK appears to be a model surveillance society.
    (C) Surveillance society is a topic of some contemporary films in the US and UK.
    (D) UK Internet users are relatively free from surveillance.

Summary

Read the sentences below and choose the sentence that best summarises paragraph 3.

(A) Surveillance society is a troubling development in the advanced Western democracies.

(B) Film is one reflection of our society's obsession with prying into the lives of others.

(C) Films have frequently depicted the disturbing implications of the medium itself, by highlighting our desires to peer into the lives of those around us.

Discussion

1. Do you agree with the author that surveillance is for the most part a negative factor in modern society? Discuss some ways in which surveillance is necessary, even benevolent.

2. Discuss the following statement, taking pro and con positions: "[I]n a democracy, particularly one supposedly governed by the common law, people have the right to anonymity and privacy, even in public places." *No CCTV* HP <http://no-cctv.org.uk/faq.asp>

Homework / Research

2014 marks the 65th anniversary of the publication of George Orwell's *1984*. Read the novel and discuss its vision of a surveillance society.

Chapter 14

Refugees and Asylum Seekers in the UK

映画『この自由な世界で』(2007)より

Warming-Up Activities:

1. Brainstorming on the Topic

日本や他のアジア諸国での外国人労働者や移民について知っているだろうか？ 彼らはどんな困難に直面しているだろうか？

2. Vocabulary

- ☐ refugee　　　名 難民
- ☐ asylum　　　名 避難、亡命 (cf. asylum seeker)
- ☐ residence　　名 住居
- ☐ criterion　　　名 (複 –a) 基準
- ☐ exploitation　名 搾取 (他動 exploit)
- ☐ exclusion　　　名 排除 (他動 exclude)
- ☐ persecution　　名 迫害 (他動 persecute)
- ☐ margin　　　　名 周縁 (形 marginal)
- ☐ deportation　　名 国外追放、強制送還 (cf. repatriation)
- ☐ contradictory　形 矛盾する (名 contradiction)

There has been much hand-wringing in the UK about the social and economic impact of migrant workers, refugees and asylum seekers, not to mention the extension of criminal and terrorist networks into the UK. Over the last two decades, the number of foreign nationals working in the UK has risen to about 4.8 million—almost 8 percent of the total population. Of these, just over a million are from the 10 accession states that joined the European Union in 2004. Eight of these, called the A8, are former communist Eastern Bloc countries, including Poland, Czech Republic, Estonia and Hungary.

The expansion of the EU has been keenly felt in the UK where, under a Worker Registration Scheme, A8 nationals are allowed free entry, unlimited stay and the promise of residence after 12 months of uninterrupted work. EU membership for these countries has been conditional on meeting the so-called Copenhagen criteria, namely, democratic reforms and respect for human rights. Ironically, once reaching the UK, these foreign workers often face exploitation, poverty and social exclusion. The UK's "open door" for foreign labour is, however, not accorded asylum seekers, refugees fleeing persecution in their home countries, who are awaiting judgement on staying in the UK. In 2010 about 18,000 applications for asylum were received in the UK, 74 percent of which were rejected. While many return to face possible violence or persecution, others choose to remain illegally in the UK, cast to margins of society, sometimes economically exploited and living in fear of deportation.

While foreign workers and asylum seekers frequently draw anger in the British press, so also do films play on British fears of foreign intruders. *Children of Men*, a film set in the year 2027 about human infertility caused by environmental pollution, offers disturbing scenes of immigrants and refugees penned up like human cattle. Here is a UK in chaos, overrun by immigrants. Similar anxieties, following the collapse of the Soviet Union, are part of *Eastern Promises*, a film about the Russian mafia in London. Second-generation Russian immigrant and mid-wife Anna comes into possession of the diary of a murdered Russian prostitute, and is drawn into the mafia underworld as she tries to protect the infant born to the woman. The film stirs fears of lawless and unassimilable foreigners.

映画『イースタン・プロミス』(2007) より

A more sympathetic view is offered in *It's a Free World* (2007), which sheds light on the situation of A8 nationals and asylum seekers. The main character Angie works for a recruitment company operating in Eastern Europe. [A] Fired from her job after she is sexually harassed by her boss, she teams up with her flat-mate Rosie to form their own agency, handing out work to foreign workers in the parking space behind a local pub. [B] Angie wants the best for her son Jamie, and she believes she is helping those around her. [C] Angie opens her home to Mahmood and his family, refugees who have been refused asylum and have gone into hiding because return to Iran would mean imprisonment or death. [D] However, after getting Mahmood a job and a fake passport, she unintentionally betrays the family through one of her schemes. While Angie's actions are at times admirable, and her situation as a single working-mother sympathetic, her character shows the contradictory impulses of white Britons in this new "free" world.

Notes

- l. 7: **Eastern Bloc** 東側（冷戦時代の共産圏） ● l. 8: **EU** ヨーロッパ共同体
- l. 8-9: **WorkerRegistration Scheme** 労働者登録制度 ● l. 11: **conditional** 形 (on ~)次第である
- l. 11: **Copenhagen criteria** コペンハーゲン基準（ある国が EU に加盟できるかどうかの基準）
- l. 14: **accorded > accord** 他動 (…に)~を授ける ● l. 21: **intruders > intruder** 名 侵入者 ● l. 22: **infertility** 名 不妊、子供が生まれないこと ● l. 24: **overrun** 他動 ~を侵略させる、(受け身で be overrun by/with ~で)覆われる ● l. 24-25: **the Soviet Union** ソビエト連邦 ● l. 27: **prostitute** 名 娼婦 ● l. 27: **underworld** 名 地下世界、暗黒街 ● l. 30: **unassimilable** ⇔ **assimilable** と考えよ

Comprehension

1. Which of the claims below is NOT made about immigrants and asylum seekers in UK films?
   (A) Most British films have avoided realistic treatment of current UK economic conditions.
   (B) Many films reflect the anxieties of the post-Cold War and post-9/11 era.
   (C) Some films show the dangers of crime associated with immigrants and foreign workers.
   (D) While some films play on fear, others give a realistic view of the refugees and foreign workers.

2. The phrase hand-wringing in paragraph 1 is closest in meaning to
   (A) hard labour   (B) concern
   (C) anger   (D) support

3. Which of the facts below is NOT true of refugees and asylum seekers in the UK?
   (A) The system for accepting refugees to the UK was set up in 2004.
   (B) Asylum seekers are refugees awaiting judgement of their entry to the UK.
   (C) The majority of 2010 applications were rejected.
   (D) Asylum seekers may face danger if they are forced to return to their home countries.

4. Which of the claims below is NOT true of the films discussed in paragraph 2?
   (A) Foreign intruders are part of the dystopian vision of *Children of Men*.
   (B) Much like the press, recent films play on fears around foreign nationals in the UK.
   (C) *Eastern Promises* reflects anxieties about foreign crime networks operating in the UK.
   (D) Both *Children of Men* and *Eastern Promises* focus on the situation of illegal foreign workers in the UK.

5. The word keenly in paragraph 2 is closest in meaning to
   (A) strongly   (B) earnestly
   (C) painfully   (D) emotionally

6. Which of the facts below is NOT true of foreign workers in the UK?
    (A) The number of foreign nationals working in the UK has increased over the last 20 years or so.
    (B) About 70 percent of A8 nationals are rejected entry each year.
    (C) Some foreign workers may be eligible to stay in the UK on a permanent basis.
    (D) Foreign workers make up close to 8% of the UK population.

7. [A], [B], [C] and [D] indicate where the following sentence can be added to paragraph 4. Mark the answer on your answer sheet.
    Yet the lure of money takes over, resulting in the neglect of her son, the alienation of parents and friends, and the endangerment of those she seeks to protect.

8. Which of the following facts or claims can NOT be found of the film *It's a Free World*?
    (A) The actions of main character Angie are often contradictory.
    (B) Angie and Rose are lured by money into illegal activities.
    (C) Angie shows herself capable of balancing work and family in her new career.
    (D) Angie loses her job after she is harassed.

9. Which of the following facts or claims can be found in the essay?
    (A) There is concern about foreign workers, crime networks and terrorism in the UK today.
    (B) The character of Angie in *It's a Free World* is roundly condemned.
    (C) Acts of kindness and charity are good ways to help foreign workers and asylum seekers.
    (D) UK immigration policy is consistent with its stance on democratic and social reform in the EU.

10. The phrase sheds light on in paragraph 4 is closest in meaning to
    (A) helps to explain   (B) includes
    (C) covers over   (D) turns on

Summary

Read the sentences below and choose the sentence that best summarises paragraph 2.

(A) The number of foreign nationals in the UK is increasing each year.

(B) The UK has distinct and contradictory policies for dealing with foreign workers and refugee claimants.

(C) The UK maintains an open door policy on immigration and refugee claimants.

Discussion

Discuss the contradictory behaviour of Angie, as presented in the passage. Is hers a natural response? What actions would you take on a personal or social level to help such people in need?

Homework / Research

1. Research the situation of asylum seekers in the UK using the UN Refugee Agency HP: <http://www.unhcr.org.uk/about-us/the-uk-and-asylum.html>. Where do asylum seekers come from and how does the UK compare with other countries for accepting such refugees?

2. Watch other films that deal with immigrants, foreign workers and terrorist networks in the UK, including *Dirty Pretty Things*, *Four Lions* and *Closed Circuit*. Do these films stoke fears about foreigners or do they help illuminate their social and economic situation?

Chapter 15

Not Always What It Seems:
England in Irish Films

映画『麦の穂をゆらす風』(2006)より

Warming-Up Activities:

1. Brainstorming on the Topic

アイルランドについて何を知っているだろう？　アイルランドと聞いて連想する人物、場所、物、イベントや歴史的事件などのリストを作ってみよう。クラスメートのリストと比較してみよう。

2. Vocabulary

☐ euphemistically	名 婉曲的に(名 euphemism)	☐ cause	名 原因、大義
☐ hostility	名 敵意、(複数で)交戦状態(形 hostile)	☐ ambivalent	形 両面価値的な
☐ dominate	他動 〜を支配する	☐ attain	他動 〜を達成する、〜に到達する
☐ oppressor	名 抑圧者(cf. oppression, oppress)	☐ allegiance	名 (主君や国家への)忠誠
☐ commit	他動 〜を託す、〜を(to…に)専心させる	☐ surpass	他動 〜をしのぐ、超える

Reading

映画『マイケル・コリンズ』(1996)より

The more than seven hundred years of British rule of Ireland can seem like one long progression of conflict, rebellion, and bloodshed culminating in the events of the Easter Rising of 1916, the Irish War of Independence, the ensuing Irish Civil War, and the establishment of a divided Ireland (the loyalist North and the independent Republic) which set the stage for thirty more years of sectarian violence erupting in the late 1960s, euphemistically known as the "Troubles".

It should come as no surprise that Irish versus British and Republican versus Loyalist hostilities are at the centre of much of Irish cinema. After all, conflict makes for good drama, as seen in such films as *In the Name of the Father* (1993), *Michael Collins* (1996), and *The Wind That Shakes the Barley* (2006). However, the image of an unrelenting Irish march towards freedom simplifies a more complex history. In *The Story of Ireland*, the BBC companion series to the book of the same title, Fergal Keane explains that Irish rebellions in the 17th and 18th centuries more often wanted "home rule" within the United Kingdom rather than independence. The 19th century, especially, was a world dominated by the British Empire, and an Irishman could do worse than making a career for himself as a bureaucrat in Her Majesty's Civil Service or as a soldier in the Royal Irish Constabulary. A narrative of English oppressors and Irish victims drawn along clear lines of demarcation is simple and dramatic, but the reality is more complicated.

One film that depicts the ambiguity of the interrelated history of Ireland and England in surprising and subtle ways is Neil Jordan's *The Crying Game* (1992), an Irish movie directed by an Irishman and produced in England. Film critic Harlan Kennedy describes *The Crying Game* as a movie in which "everything is not what it seems."

The movie begins when Jody, a British soldier stationed in Northern Ireland during the "Troubles", is abducted by members of the IRA. The irony is that Jody is of West Indian heritage, a postcolonial subject serving to maintain control in another former British colony. Among Jody's captors is Fergus, a half-hearted IRA soldier committed to the cause but ambivalent about the means of attaining it. Fergus cannot help but see Jody as a man rather than the enemy. For his kindness to Jody, Fergus is reprimanded and ordered to take Jody into the woods and shoot him. Fortunately, Fergus's humanity trumps his sense of national identity and political allegiance.

In one of the movie's first ironic turns, Jody, knowing it's not in Fergus's nature to kill a man, attempts to escape, only to be run over and killed by a British armoured vehicle. [A] The irony continues as Fergus, now in peril for his life, flees "across the water" to England, hoping to hide from the IRA for whom he is now a target. [B] Out of grief and guilt, Fergus finds Dil, the girlfriend Jody has told him about. United through their shared grief, they eventually fall in love. Fergus, though, has kept his IRA connection a secret from Dil. However, in a movie where nothing is what it seems, Dil also has a secret of her own which Fergus discovers only when he sees her naked for the first time—Dil is a male transvestite. "She" is a "he". [C] However, just as his humanity previously surpassed his national identity, it now overrides his sexual identity and puts everything into question. [D] As the gender scholar Judith Halberstam notes, "the fact that Dil is anatomically male throws all other identities in the film into doubt." In the case of the image of England in Irish film, it isn't always as it seems.

Notes

- l. 8: **sectarian** 形 宗派(党派)の、宗派(党派)による内部分裂の
- l. 10-11: **Republican and Loyalist** アイルランド共和国独立を応援する立場とイギリス国王への忠誠を守る立場
- l. 14: **unrelenting** 形 容赦しない
- l. 19: **Her Majesty's Civil Service** イギリスの内閣、もしくは国家公務員の総称
- l. 20: **the Royal Irish Constabulary** 王立アイルランド警察隊(19世紀から1922年まで存在)
- l. 21: **demarcation** 名 境界、限界
- l. 28: **abduct** 他動 ～を誘拐する
- l. 28: **the IRA** アイルランド共和国軍(南北アイルランド統一を目指す過激派組織)
- l. 29: **West Indian** カリブ地域の(West Indies は「カリブ諸島」)
- l. 29: **postcolonial** 形 ポストコロニアルの、植民地主義以降の、旧植民地の
- l. 33: **reprimanded > reprimand** 他動 ～を叱責する
- l. 43: **transvestite** 名 服装倒錯者
- l. 44: **overrides > override** 他動 ～を覆す、～に優先する
- l. 46: **anatomically** 副 解剖学的に (名 anatomy 形 anatomical)

Comprehension

1. According to the essay, what is the best description of the history of Ireland and England?
   (A) It is a simple story of good versus evil.
   (B) It is a very long and complex story.
   (C) Their histories are basically unrelated.
   (D) Their histories are essentially the same.

2. According to the essay, which of the following statements is true about Fergal Keane?
   (A) He is the narrator of *The Story of Ireland*.
   (B) He favours "home rule" for Ireland.
   (C) He is the director of *Michael Collins*.
   (D) He is a British bureaucrat.

3. The expression culminating in in paragraph 1 is closest in meaning to
   (A) beginning with
   (B) avoiding
   (C) opposing
   (D) leading up to

4. The author cites the films *In the Name of the Father, Michael Collins,* and *The Wind That Shakes the Barley* as examples of
   (A) BBC documentaries about Irish history.
   (B) Irish films which focus on aspects of Irish/British conflict.
   (C) British films which focus on Irish immigration to England.
   (D) movies about the British empire in the 19th century.

5. The expression could do worse than in paragraph 2 is closest in meaning to
   (A) would regret
   (B) would do worse by
   (C) would do well by
   (D) would not think of

6. The author cites Harlan Kennedy as an example of:
   (A) someone who knows about Irish films.
   (B) an Irish film director.
   (C) someone who believes that "everything is not what it seems."
   (D) a friend of Neil Jordan's.

7. The expression half-hearted in paragraph 4 is closest in meaning to
   (A) unhealthy
   (B) confused
   (C) unenthusiastic
   (D) overworked

8. The essay implies that after discovering Dil's secret,
   (A) Fergus realises he has never loved Dil.
   (B) Fergus is confused but still loves Dil.
   (C) Fergus will soon be returning to Ireland.
   (D) Fergus wishes that Jody was still alive.

9. [A], [B], [C] and [D] indicate where the following sentence can be added to paragraph 5. Mark your answer on your answer sheet.
   Fergus's initial reactions are anger and disgust.

10. The essay implies that *The Crying Game* is unusual because
    (A) it manages to avoid making any references to the Irish/British conflict.
    (B) of the unusual way it suggests the complex nature of Irish/British relations.
    (C) it focuses on a love story between a man from Ireland and a woman from England.
    (D) of its graphic portrayal of violence between Irish nationalists and British loyalists.

Summary

Read the sentences below and choose the statement that best summarises the main idea of paragraph 2.

(A) A narrative of victims versus oppressors is a clear way to understand Irish history.

(B) The best Irish films are those that focus on the conflict between Ireland and England.

(C) The history of the relation between Ireland and England is not a simple one.

Discussion

1. Do you feel the author provides an accurate account of the debate regarding the history of Irish/British relations? Draw on your knowledge of films, current events, or novels to support your view.

2. What are some ways in which television, movies, and other media simplify conflict between different countries? Can you think of some examples from current news? Brainstorm and discuss what you know about these issues.

Homework / Research

Watch the movie *The Crying Game*. Be prepared to discuss the issues the movie deals with. What do you think of the movie? How does it compare with the views expressed in the essay? Watch one of the other movies referred to in the essay (*In the Name of the Father*, *Michael Collins*, or *The Wind That Shakes the Barley*). How does it compare with *The Crying Game*? Be prepared to explain your views.

人名・映画作品・企業名など

Chapter 1

Harry Potter ハリー・ポッター。イギリスの作家J・K・ローリング（J. K. Rowling, 1965～）の連作児童文学の主人公。ホグワーツ魔法学校に入学し、友人たちと様々な冒険を経て、最終的に自分の両親を殺した悪の魔法使いヴォルデモートに立ち向かう。作品の邦題は、それぞれ『ハリー・ポッターと賢者の石』、『ハリー・ポッターと秘密の部屋』、『ハリー・ポッターとアズカバンの囚人』、『ハリー・ポッターと炎のゴブレット』、『ハリー・ポッターと不死鳥の騎士団』、『ハリー・ポッターと謎のプリンス』、『ハリー・ポッターと死の秘宝』となる。

Charles Perrault シャルル・ペロー（1628～1703）。フランスの詩人。古典より現代文学が優れているとして古今論争を起こすが、フランス国外では一般におとぎ話の編纂者として知られる。

The Secret Garden 『秘密の花園』（1911）。イギリス人作家（のちにアメリカに移住）フランシス・ホジソン・バーネット（Frances Hodgson Burnett, 1849～1924）の代表的作品。植民地インド育ちの主人公が、両親の死を機にイギリスの叔父の家に引き取られる。そこで悲しみに心を閉ざした叔父や同じく親の愛を知らない従弟の心を開いていく。1993年に同名で映画化されている。

The Chronicles of Narnia 『ナルニア国ものがたり』。イギリスの作家C・S・ルイス（C. S. Lewis, 1898～1963）の連作児童文学。架空の世界ナルニアを舞台に、20世紀イギリスから入ってきたピーター、スーザン、エドマンド、ルーシーの4人姉妹が、世界の正統な王である、ライオンのアスランに王位を取り戻すべく奔走する。いたるところにキリスト教の寓意がちりばめられていることでも知られる。邦題は『ライオンと魔女』、『カスピアン王子のつのぶえ』、『朝びらき丸東の海へ』、『銀のいす』、『馬と少年』、『魔術師のおい』、『さいごの戦い』。

His Dark Materials 『ライラの冒険』。イギリスの作家フィリップ・プルマン（Philip Pullman, 1946～）による連作児童文学。我々の世界とは異なる世界に住む主人公の少女ライラが、我々の世界に住む少年ウィルとともに異世界間を移動するパラレル・ワールド物語。ただし、本文でも触れられている通り、キリスト教批判と受け取れる箇所が多く、北米ではボイコットを受けている。邦題は『黄金の羅針盤』、『神秘の短剣』、『琥珀の望遠鏡』。なお、シリーズのタイトルはジョン・ミルトン（John Milton, 1608～74）『失楽園』（*Paradise Lost*, 1667）から取られている。プルマンは無神論者としても有名で、ルイスを手厳しく批判している。

Alice's Adventures in Wonderland 『不思議の国のアリス』。イギリスの作家・数学者ルイス・キャロル（Lewis Carroll, 1832～98）の書いた小説。少女アリスが白ウサギを追いかけて巨大なウサギ穴に落ち、そこから奇妙な体験をする物語。

The Lord of the Rings 『指輪物語』（映画シリーズのタイトルは『ロード・オブ・ザ・リング』）。イギリスの作家J・R・R・トールキン（J. R. R. Tolkien, 1892～1973）の連作ファンタジー小説。人間より小さく牧歌的な暮らしを営むホビット、美しく力も強いが滅び行く定めにあるエルフ、エルフが堕落して醜い姿となったオークなどがいる昔の世界。すべてを支配する指輪の持ち主となってしまったホビットのフロド・バギンズは、指輪が冥王サウロンの手に渡る前に滅びの山に捨てるための旅に出る。このプロットを軸に、様々な種族の中から人間が台頭してきた経緯などが壮大に描かれる。邦題は、『旅の仲間』、『二つの塔』、『王の帰還』。

Chapter 2

Sunday Bloody Sunday 映画『日曜日は別れの時』（1971）。若い両性愛の芸術家と中年男性医師、若いビジネスウーマンとの三角関係を描いた作品。監督：ジョン・シュレシンジャー。

My Beautiful Laundrette 映画『マイ・ビューティフル・ランドレット』（1985）。ビジネスで成功しようとするパキスタン系の若者と白人至上主義のグループに入っていた白人の若者との同性愛を描く。監督：スティーヴン・フレアーズ、脚本：ハニフ・クレイシ、主演：ダニエル・デイ・ルイス。

Thatcher マーガレット・サッチャー（1925～2013）。イギリスの保守党政治家、首相（1979～90）。イギリスで女性初の首相で、市場経済重視、対外強硬主義、公共事業・福祉の削減などを特徴とすることから「鉄の女」（the Iron Lady）と呼ばれる。

Sally Potter サリー・ポッター（1949～）。イギリスの映画監督。代表作に『オルランド』（1992）、『タンゴ・レッスン』（1997）、『耳に残るは君の歌声』（2000）など。

Orlando 映画『オルランド』（1992）。原作はイギリスの作家ヴァージニア・ウルフ（Virginia Woolf, 1882～1941）の同名の小説（1928）。時代と性別を越えて生きるオルランドを主人公とする幻想小説だが、映画ではオルランドの人生が1990年代まで延ばされている。監督：サリー・ポッター、主演：ティルダ・スウィントン。

Tilda Swinton ティルダ・スウィントン（1960～）。イギリスの女優。1980年代後半からアート系作品にも多く出演し、近年では『ナルニア国物語』のシリーズの悪役「白い魔女」ジャディス役で知られる。代表作に『ラスト・オブ・イングランド』（1988）、『エドワード2世』（1991）、『オルランド』（1992）、『ビーチ』（2000）、『ナルニア国物語──ライオンと魔女』（2005）など。

Lilting 映画『リルティング』（2014）。一人息子を亡くしたカンボジア系移民の母が、その息子の男性の恋人とともにその悲しみを乗り越えていく物語。2014年現在、本邦未公開。監督：ホン・カウ、主演：ベン・ウィショー。

Victim 映画『犠牲者』（1961）。"homosexual"という単語を初めて使った映画作品とされる。2014年現在、本邦未公開。主演：ダーク・ボガード。

Dirk Bogarde ダーク・ボガード（1921～99）。イギリスの俳優。特にイタリアの名監督ルキノ・ヴィスコンティ（Luchino Visconti, 1906～76）の作品での出演で知られる。代表作に『二都物語』（1957）、『ダーリング』（1965）、『地獄に堕ちた勇者ども』（1969）、『ベニスに死す』（1971）、『愛の嵐』（1973）など。

Chapter 3

Queen Elizabeth II　エリザベス2世（1926～）。イギリスの女王（1952～）。イギリス連邦諸国の女王であり、国家元首でもある。ウィンザー朝で4代目に当たる。夫はデンマークおよびノルウェー王室のエディンバラ公フィリップ王配（1921～）。

The Queen　映画『クイーン』（2006）。ダイアナ元皇太子の交通事故からその葬儀に至るまでのイギリス王室の人間模様を描いた作品。主演：ヘレン・ミレン。

Princess Diana　ダイアナ元皇太子妃（1961～97）。イギリスの貴族の生まれ。チャールズ皇太子と結婚し、ふたりの子供を授かる（詳細は本文参照）。

Tony Blair　トニー・ブレア（1953～）。イギリスの労働党政治家。首相（1997～2007）。メディア戦略にたけ、圧倒的な支持率を誇るが、在任期間後期は求心力を失う。

Prince Charles　チャールズ皇太子（1948～）。エリザベス2世の長男。ダイアナと知り合う以前から交際のあったカミラ・パーカー・ボウルズ（現コーンウォール公爵夫人カミラ、1947～）との不倫は、離婚の大きな原因とされる。2005年にカミラと結婚。

Prince William　ウィリアム王子（1982～）。チャールズ皇太子の長男。ケンブリッジ公爵。現時点で王位継承順位2位。

Catherine Middleton　キャサリン・ミドルトン、現ケンブリッジ公爵夫人キャサリン（1982～）。2010年にウィリアム王子と婚約。翌年に盛大な結婚式が開かれた。

Roman Holiday　映画『ローマの休日』（1953）。架空の王国のアン王女を主人公としたロマンティック・コメディ。王室の堅苦しい生活に嫌気がさしたアンがローマでこっそり抜け出し、はじめはスクープ記事を書くつもりで接近したアメリカ人新聞記者ジョーと楽しい休日を過ごす。その後、アン王女は王女としての自覚に目覚め、ふたりは思い出を胸に秘めて別れる。主演：オードリー・ヘップバーン、グレゴリー・ペック。

Audrey Hepburn　オードリー・ヘップバーン（1929～93）。イギリス人の父とオランダ人の母を持つ、ハリウッド黄金期を代表する女優。『ローマの休日』（1953）をはじめ、『麗しのサブリナ』（1954）、『ティファニーで朝食を』（1961）、『シャレード』（1963）、『マイ・フェア・レディ』（1964）など多数の映画に出演。その後女優を引退し、1988年からユニセフ親善大使として世界各国で人道的活動に力を入れる。

Unlawful Killing　ドキュメンタリー映画『不法な殺人』（2011）。ダイアナ元皇太子妃の恋人だったドディ・アルファイド（1955～97）の遺族の援助のもと、ダイアナ元皇太子妃およびドディ・アルファイド他殺説を立証しようとしたドキュメンタリーで、2011年のカンヌ映画祭に出品されたものの、公開は中止となった。このことが様々な憶測を呼んでいる。

The Queen and I　スー・タウンゼント（Sue Townsend, 1946～2014）の小説『女王様と私』（1992）。イギリスで王制が廃止されたという設定のもと、バッキンガム宮殿を追われて庶民の生活をしなければならなくなったロイヤル・ファミリー（実名で登場）を描く。タウンゼントはラジオおよびテレビドラマのエイドリアン・モールのシリーズを書いたことで有名。

Queen Camilla　スー・タウンゼントの小説『カミラ女王』（2006）。『女王様と私』の続編。

Diana　映画『ダイアナ』（2013）。ダイアナ元皇太子妃の最後の2年間を描いた伝記映画。批評家の評価は高いとは言えず、商業的にも成功とは言えない作品だった。主演：ナオミ・ワッツ。

Chapter 4

Room at the Top　映画『年上の女(ひと)』（1959）。ジョン・ブレイン（John Braine, 1922～86）による同名の小説（1957）を映画化した作品（詳細は本文参照）。主演：ローレンス・ハーヴェイ、シモーヌ・シニョレ。

Look Back in Anger　映画『怒りをこめて振り返れ』（1959）。ジョン・オズボーン（John Osborne, 1929～94）による同名の戯曲（1956）を映画化した作品（詳細は本文参照）。監督：トニー・リチャードソン。

A Taste of Honey　映画『蜜の味』（1961）。シーラ・ディレイニー（Shelagh Delaney, 1938～2011）による同名の戯曲（1958）を映画化した作品（詳細は本文参照）。

Brighton Rock　映画『ブライトン・ロック』（2010）。グレアム・グリーン（Graham Greene, 1904～91）の同名の小説（1938）を映画化した作品。原作は10代のギャングを扱った小説でありながら、作者のカトリック信仰と罪の意識の問題が扱われていることでも知られ、これまでにも何度か映画化やTVドラマ化が試みられている。主演：サム・ライリー。

NEDs　映画『ネッズ』（2010）。1970年代のスコットランド、グラスゴーを舞台に、労働者階級出身の少年の成長を描く（詳細は本文参照）。監督は『戦火の馬』（2011）などで俳優として知られるピーター・マラン。

It's a Free World　映画『この自由な世界で』（2007）。ふたりの若い女性が自らの派遣会社を設立するが、次第にひとりが法の抜け道を通って、他者を搾取するような禁断のビジネスに手を染めてしまう（詳細は本文参照）。監督：ケン・ローチ。

Happy-Go-Lucky　映画『ハッピー・ゴー・ラッキー』（2008）。若い女性小学校教師が一念発起して自動車の免許を取ろうとすると、これまで見えてこなかった人生の側面が見えてくる。監督：マイク・リー、主演：サリー・ホーキンス。

The Selfish Giant　映画『わがままな大男』（2013）。アイルランドの小説家・劇作家オスカー・ワイルド（Oscar Wilde, 1854～1900）の同名の短編小説（1888）を元に、大胆なアレンジを加えた作品。子供と巨人は、北イングランドの工業都市で電線などを盗んで売る社会の最下層の少年たちと廃品回収業者に置き換えられている。

Chapter 5

Frank Lampard　フランク・ランパード（1978～）。イギリスを代表するサッカー選手。ポジションはミッドフィールダー。ロンドンのチ

ェルシーFCで長年プレイし、クラブで通算最多得点記録を持つ。イングランド代表にも選出される。父もサッカー選手だった。

Monty Python イギリスのお笑いグループ。グレアム・チャップマン(Graham Chapman, 1941〜89)、ジョン・クリーズ(John Cleese, 1939〜)、エリック・アイドル(Eric Idle, 1943〜)、テリー・ジョーンズ(Terry Jones, 1942〜)、マイケル・ペイリン(Michael Palin, 1943〜)という5人にアメリカ人のアニメーター、テリー・ギリアム(Terry Gilliam, 1940〜:のちにイギリスに帰化)を加えた6人組。彼らの番組『空飛ぶモンティ・パイソン』(Monty Python's Flying Circus)は、シュールな笑いやブラック・ユーモアを特徴とし、イギリスで多大な影響力を持った。

Proust マルセル・プルースト(Marcel Proust, 1871〜1922)。フランスの小説家。自分の分身である作家の精神遍歴を描いた『失われた時を求めて』(In Search of Lost Time/仏 À la recherche du temps perdu, 1913〜27)は現代文学の最高傑作のひとつとされる。最も長い小説のひとつでもあり、語り手が急に過去の記憶にとらわれること(とりわけ紅茶に浸したマドレーヌから過去の記憶が蘇ることは有名)によって物語が中断されることはよく知られている。

Fever Pitch 映画『ぼくのプレミア・ライフ』(1997)。原作はイギリスの作家ニック・ホーンビィ(Nick Hornby, 1957〜)の自伝的作品(1992)で、ロンドンのサッカー・チーム、アーセナルFCの熱烈なサポーターの生活を描いたもの。同じ原作で、舞台をアメリカ、スポーツを野球に置き換えたアメリカ版の映画もあるので注意(邦題は『2番目のキス』(2005))。主演:コリン・ファース。

My Name Is Joe 映画『マイ・ネーム・イズ・ジョー』(1998)。スコットランドを舞台にし、失業中でアルコール依存症に悩む主人公が友人とサッカー・チームを作る。監督:ケン・ローチ。

Purely Belter 映画『シーズン・チケット』(2000)。イングランド北部のニューカッスルを舞台に、地元チーム、ニューカッスル・ユナイテッドの熱烈なサッカー・ファンの少年たちを描く。

Bend It Like Beckham 映画『ベッカムに恋して』(2002)。ディヴィッド・ベッカム(David Beckham, 1975〜)のようなサッカー選手になりたいと思うインド系移民の少女の物語(邦題は誤解を招くので注意)。西ロンドンが舞台。主演:パーミンダー・ナグラ、キーラ・ナイトレー。

Green Street 映画『フーリガン』(2005)。ロンドンのイースト・エンドのチーム、ウェスト・ハム・ユナイテッドのフーリガンたちを、不当な理由でエリートの道から落伍したアメリカ人学生の視点から描く。主演:イライジャ・ウッド。

The Damned United 映画『くたばれ!ユナイテッド』(2009)。原作は2006年刊。弱小チームを率いてリーグ戦やカップ線を制覇するなど、輝かしい戦績を残したサッカーの名監督ブライアン・クラフ(Brian Clough, 1935〜2004)の監督就任当初の苦難を描く。主演:マイケル・シーン。

Chapter 6

Margaret Thatcher Chapter 2の注釈を参照。

Alan Bennett アラン・ベネット(1934〜)。イギリスの劇作家・脚本家。『英国万歳』(The Madness of George III, 1991 [劇]; The Madness of King George, 1994 [映画])で有名。

The History Boys 戯曲『ヒストリー・ボーイズ』(2004)およびその映画化作品(2006)。北イングランドの公立学校を舞台にした物語(詳細は本文参照)。映画版では、本邦ではハリー・ポッター作品のダーズリー役で知られるリチャード・グリフィスが、ヘクター先生役を好演している。本邦では、2014年に松坂桃季、中村倫也主演で上演され、話題となる。

Harry Potter and the Order of the Phoenix 小説『ハリー・ポッターと不死鳥の騎士団』(2003)およびその映画化作品(2007)。ハリー・ポッターの5作目に当たるこの作品では、本文の通り魔法省から派遣されたアンブリッジ先生が登場する。

Goodbye, Mr. Chips 映画『チップス先生さようなら』(1969)。1934年に出版されたジェイムズ・ヒルトン(James Hilton, 1900〜54)の同名の中編小説のミュージカル映画。パブリック・スクール(名門私立校)の古風なラテン語教師の半生を描く。主演:ピーター・オトゥール。

Another Country 映画『アナザー・カントリー』(1984)。1930年代のパブリック・スクール(イートン校がモデル)を舞台に、同性愛ゆえに監督生になれず、エリート・コースから外れて挫折を味わう青年の物語。主人公のガイ・ベネットは実在のスパイ、ガイ・バージェス(1911〜63)をモデルにしている。主演:ルパート・エヴェレット、コリン・ファース。

If . . . 映画『ifもしも…』(1968)。1960年代のパブリック・スクールを舞台とし、監督生の体罰、下級生使役などをブラック・ユーモアで諷刺した作品。賛否両論があった。監督:リンゼイ・アンダーソン。

Melody 映画『小さな恋のメロディ』(1971)。公立学校を舞台とした作品。比較的裕福な家庭に育つダニエルが、貧しいが温かい家庭に育つ少女メロディと幼い恋に落ちる。本国より日本でヒットした。

Chapter 7

Oh! What a Lovely War 映画『素晴らしき戦争』(1969)。第一次世界大戦を描いた同名のミュージカル(1963)を原作とした作品。監督:リチャード・アッテンボロー、主演:ダーク・ボガード、ジョン・ギールグッド。

Blackadder TV番組『ブラックアダー』(1983〜89)。イギリス史の様々な場面を切り取り、そこでイギリスの俳優・コメディアン、ローワン・アトキンソン(Rowan Atkinson, 1955〜)が演じる毒舌家のエドマンド・ブラックアダーと、間の抜けたボールドリックの活躍を描いたコメディ。

Mr. Bean TV番組『Mr.ビーン』(1990〜95)。ローワン・アトキンソンが演じるMr.ビーンが自分勝手で、子供っぽい行動が引き起こす騒動を描くコメディで、ウィットのあるせりふを特徴とする『ブラックアダー』とは対照的に、せりふはほとんどない。日本でもNHKで放映され、ブームとなった。

Chapter 8

the Who ザ・フー。ロジャー・ダルトリー(Roger Daltrey, 1944～)とピート・タウンゼント(Pete Townshend, 1945～)を中心に、1964年に結成されたイギリスのロックバンド。ザ・ビートルズ(the Beatles)、ザ・ローリング・ストーンズ(the Rolling Stones)、ザ・キンクス(the Kinks)と並んでブリティッシュ・ロックで最も影響力の大きいバンドのひとつ。代表曲に「マイ・ジェネレーション」("My Generation", 1965)、「サブスティチュート」(発売当初の邦題は「恋のピンチヒッター」、"Substitute", 1966)など。

the Beatles ザ・ビートルズ。世界で最も有名なイギリスのロックバンド(結成は1960年、解散は1970年)。イングランド北部の港町リヴァプール出身のジョン・レノン(John Lennon, 1940～80)、ポール・マッカートニー(Paul McCartney, 1942～)、ジョージ・ハリスン(George Harrison, 1943～2001)、リンゴ・スター(Ringo Starr, 1940～)の4人。代表曲には「抱きしめたい」("I Want to Hold Your Hand", 1963)、「ハード・デイズ・ナイト」(日本発売当初の邦題は「ビートルズがやって来た、ヤア、ヤア、ヤア」、"A Hard Day's Night", 1964)、「ヘイ・ジュード」("Hey Jude", 1968)、「レット・イット・ビー」("Let It Be", 1970)など数多く、ファッションでも一世を風靡し、全世界で「ビートルマニア」(Beatlemania)と呼ばれるブームを巻き起こした。

Mary Quant マリー・クワント(1934～)。イギリスのファッション・デザイナーで、1960年代にミニスカートを全世界的に流行させたことで有名。なお、日本では「マリー・クワント」として知られているが、英語の発音としては「メアリー・クウォント」に近い(/ˈmeəriˈkwɒnt/)。

Brighton Rock Chapter 4の注釈を参照。

Quadrophenia 映画『さらば青春の光』(1979)。ザ・フーの同名のロック・オペラ(1973)を翻案した映画作品(ただし、ザ・フーのアルバムの邦題は『四重人格』)。当時のモッズの生き方やファッションを蘇らせた作品として知られる。主演:フィル・ダニエルズ。

the Jam ザ・ジャム。1972～82年に活躍したイギリスのロックバンド。後述のポール・ウェラーを中心としたバンドで、特にモッズのリバイバルに貢献した。代表曲に「ゴーイング・アンダーグラウンド」("Going Underground", 1980)など。

Paul Weller ポール・ウェラー(1958～)。イギリスのロック・ミュージシャン、作曲家。ザ・ジャムおよびスタイル・カウンシル(The Style Council, 1983～89)といったバンドで中心的な役割を果たして多くの楽曲を残し、2014年現在ではソロ活動をしている。

the Kinks ザ・キンクス。レイ・デイヴィス(Ray Davies, 1944～)とデイヴ・デイヴィス(Dave Davies, 1947～)を中心に、1963年に結成されたイギリスのロックバンド。代表曲に「ユー・リアリー・ガット・ミー」("You Really Got Me", 1964)、「ウォータールー・サンセット」("Waterloo Sunset", 1967)など。

Ray Davies レイ・デイヴィス(1944～)。イギリスのロック・ミュージシャン、作曲家。キンクスでは中心的な役割を果たし、多くの楽曲を残している。ウィットの効いたユーモアでも有名。

Oasis オアシス。ノエル・ギャラガー(Noel Gallagher, 1967～)およびリーアム・ギャラガー(Liam Gallagher, 1972～)を中心に、1991年にイングランド北部マンチェスターで結成されたロックバンド。ビートルズの再来とも呼ばれ、1990年代のチャートを後述のブラーと二分した。代表曲に「ドント・ルック・バック・イン・アンガー」("Don't Look Back in Anger", 1995)など。

Blur ブラー。デイモン・アルバーン(Damon Albarn, 1968～)を中心に、1988年にロンドンで結成されたロックバンド。ミドルクラスでウィットに富んだ曲調を特徴とし、オアシスと対照をなしていた。代表曲に「カントリー・ハウス」("Country House", 1995)など。

Suede スエード。1989年にロンドンで結成されたロックバンド。ボーカルのブレット・アンダーソン(Brett Anderson, 1967～)の両性具有的な容姿と退廃的なイメージで1990年代に人気を博す。

We Are the Mods 映画『俺たちがモッズだ』(2009)。現代アメリカのロサンジェルスを舞台に、若者の成長を通してモッズ・シーンを描く。本邦未公開。

Chapter 9

William Blake ウィリアム・ブレイク(1757～1827)。イギリスのロマン派の詩人、版画家。有名な「虎」("The Tyger", 1794)を含む『無垢の歌と経験の歌』(*Songs of Innocence and of Experience*, 1794)、『天国と地獄の結婚』(*The Marriage of Heaven and Hell*, 1790～93)など独自の世界観を示す預言的作品を残す。

"Jerusalem" 賛美歌「エルサレム」。ブレイクが自著『ミルトン』(*Milton*, 1804～8)の序に書いた詩が、一般的にこのタイトルで知られ、イギリスの賛美歌となっている。ブレイクには『エルサレム』(*Jerusalem*, 1804～20)という預言的作品もあるが、これはまったく別物。

Ray Davies Chapter 8の注釈を参照。

Village Green Preservation Society キンクスのアルバム『ヴィレッジ・グリーン・プリザヴェイション・ソサエティー』(1968)。いわゆるコンセプト・アルバムの先駆け的な作品で、田舎の牧歌的な生活へのノスタルジアが特徴。正式タイトルは*The Kinks Are the Village Green Preservation Society*。

Led Zeppelin レッド・ツェッペリン。ジミー・ペイジ(Jimmy Page, 1944～)とロバート・プラント(Robert Plant, 1948～)らを中心に、1968年に結成されたイギリスのロックバンド。初期のハードロックバンドの中で、世界で最も大きな影響力を持つバンドのひとつ。代表曲に「天国への階段」("Stairway to Heaven", 1971)や「カシミール」("Kashmir", 1975)など。J. R. R. トールキンの『指輪物語』(Chapter 1参照)を題材にした歌詞の曲も多い。

Fairport Convention フェアポート・コンヴェンション。1967年に結成されたフォークロックバンド。アメリカのフォークではなく、イギリスの民謡を現代風にアレンジしたことで有名で、アルバム『リージ・アンド・リーフ』(*Liege & Lief*, 1969)はとりわけ名盤として知られる。

Jethro Tull ジェスロ・タル。イアン・アンダーソン(Ian Anderson, 1947～)を中心に、1967年に結成されたイギリスの

ロックバンド。ハードロック、ジャズ、クラシックの要素を自在に取り入れたスタイルで知られる。日本やアメリカでは、イエスの受難劇と同じタイトルを持つコンセプト・アルバム『パッション・プレイ』(*A Passion Play*, 1973)などの作品が有名だが、イギリスでは農場の生活を歌った『日曜日の印象』(*This Was*, 1968)がいまでも人気を博している。なお、バンド名は同名のイギリスの農学者(1674〜1740?)から取られている。

XTC　XTC。1976年に結成されたイギリスのロックバンド。ニューウェイブ、オルタナティヴロックに分類されるが、ポップな曲調で1990年代のいわゆるブリットポップ(Britpop)に影響を与えた。

Oasis　Chapter 8の注釈を参照。

Blur　Chapter 8の注釈を参照。

Pulp　パルプ。ジャーヴィス・コッカー(Jarvis Cocker, 1963〜)を中心に、1978年にイングランド北部のシェフィールドで結成されたロックバンド。1990年代を代表するバンドのひとつ。代表曲に「コモン・ピープル」("Common People", 1995)など。なお、コッカーは、映画『ハリー・ポッターと炎のゴブレット』(*Harry Potter and the Goblet of Fire*, 2004)の舞踏会の場面で、ウィアード・シスターズというバンドを率いて歌っている。

Upstairs, Downstairs　TVドラマ『階上と階下』(1971〜75)。第一次世界大戦から戦間期のロンドンを舞台にした上流階級と使用人の生活を描いたITV制作のTVドラマ。

Brideshead Revisited　TVドラマ『ブライズヘッドふたたび』(1981)。イーヴリン・ウォー(Evelyn Waugh, 1903〜66)の同名の小説(1945)を、グラナダTVがドラマ化した作品。主演:ジェレミー・アイアンズ。

Midsomer Murders　TVドラマ『バーナビー警部』(1997〜)。イングランドの架空の田舎町Midsomerを舞台に、トム・バーナビー警部が事件を解決していくミステリ物。ITV制作。

Downton Abbey　TVドラマ『ダウントン・アビー──貴族とメイドと相続人』(2010〜)。20世紀初頭、イングランドの上流階級の館カントリー・ハウスである「ダウントン・アビー」を舞台に、上流階級の人々、使用人たちの人間模様を描く。主演:ヒュー・ボネヴィル、マギー・スミス。

Chapter 10

Monty Python　Chapter 5の注釈を参照。

Life of Brian　映画『ライフ・オブ・ブライアン』(1979)。モンティ・パイソンが作ったコメディ映画(詳細は本文参照)。

Monty Python's Flying Circus　映画『空飛ぶモンティ・パイソン』(1969〜74)。モンティ・パイソンのお笑い番組。短いコントを矢継ぎ早に流すスタイルを採る。「死んだオウム」("The Dead Parrot")や「スペイン異端審問」("The Spanish Inquisition")など、伝説となっているコントもあり、イギリスを含めその後のお笑い番組に多大な影響を与えた。

Monty Python and the Holy Grail　映画『モンティ・パイソン・アンド・ホーリー・グレイル』(1975)。モンティ・パイソンが作ったコメディ映画。アーサー王伝説のパロディ。

Holy Flying Circus　TV番組『聖なる空飛ぶサーカス』(2011)。『ライフ・オブ・ブライアン』直後の騒動を、モンティ・パイソンへのオマージュに満ちたスタイルで描いたもの。BBC制作。

Chapter 11

A Study in Scarlet　小説『緋色の研究』(1887)。シャーロック・ホームズの記念すべき第一回登場作品。アフガニスタンの戦争で負傷したワトソン医師はイギリスに帰国し、ベイカー・ストリート221番地に間借りするホームズの助手となる。後期の作品と異なり、ホームズは非常に風変わりな探偵として描かれている。

Sir Arthur Conan Doyle　サー・アーサー・コナン・ドイル(1859〜1930)。『四つの署名』(1890)、『バスカヴィル家の犬』(1902)、『恐怖の谷』(1915)といった長編小説、「ボヘミアの醜聞」(1891)、「まだらの紐」(1892)、「最後の事件」(1893)といった短編小説に代表されるシャーロック・ホームズ作品の作者として有名。

Sherlock Holmes Baffled　アメリカの短編映画「困惑するシャーロック・ホームズ」(1900)。無声映画。現在知られている最初のシャーロック・ホームズ映画。

Adventures of Sherlock Holmes　アメリカ映画『シャーロック・ホームズの冒険』(1905)。1892年に出版された同名の短編小説集(「ボヘミアの醜聞」、「ボスコム谷の惨聞」、「まだらの紐」など所収)を映画化した最初の作品。

Basil Rathbone　ベイジル・ラスボーン(1892〜1967)。イギリスの俳優。シャーロック・ホームズ俳優として有名。代表作に『バスカヴィル家の犬』(1939)、『シャーロック・ホームズの冒険』(1939)、『シャーロック・ホームズと恐怖の声』(1943, アメリカのオリジナル作品)、『シャーロック・ホームズ殺しのドレス』(1946, アメリカのオリジナル作品)など。

Nigel Bruce　ナイジェル・ブルース(1895〜1953)。イギリスの俳優。ラスボーンと組んでワトソン役を演じたシャーロック・ホームズ作品で有名。

Jeremy Brett　ジェレミー・ブレット(1933〜95)。イギリスの俳優。シャーロック・ホームズ俳優として有名。ミュージカル映画『マイ・フェア・レディ』(1964)のフレディ役などで知られていたが、1984年から始まったグラナダTV制作のシャーロック・ホームズ・シリーズでのホームズ役で一躍有名になる。現在でもシャーロック・ホームズ俳優としては最高との評価を受けている。シリーズ後半では病魔と闘いながら演技を続けたことでも知られる。

David Burke　ディヴィッド・バーク(1934〜)。イギリスの俳優。シリーズ初期の2年間、ブレットと組んでワトソン役を演じたシャーロック・ホームズ作品で有名。

Edward Hardwicke　エドワード・ハードウィック(1932〜2011)。イギリスの俳優。バークの跡を継いで、ブレットと組んでワトソン役を演じたシャーロック・ホームズ作品で有名。

Sherlock　TVドラマ『シャーロック』(2010〜)。シャーロック・ホームズを現代に置き換えたBBCのTVドラマで、随所に原作のパロディがあったり、現代の科学や国際情勢を取り入れていることが特徴(詳細は本文参照)。

Benedict Cumberbatch　ベネディクト・カンバーバッチ（1976～）。イギリスの俳優。映画『つぐない』（2007）、『戦火の馬』（2011）、『それでも夜は明ける』（2013）などの好演もさることながら、BBCテレビ・シリーズの『シャーロック』（2010～）におけるシャーロック・ホームズ役で有名。イギリスの俳優らしく舞台俳優としてもキャリアを積んでいる。

Martin Freeman　マーティン・フリーマン（1971～）。イギリスの俳優。映画『ラブ・アクチュアリー』（2003）などに出演。『シャーロック』のワトソン役で有名。

Steven Moffat　スティーヴン・モファット（1961～）。イギリス（スコットランド）の脚本家・プロデューサー。TV番組『ドクター・フー』や『シャーロック』の脚本・制作で有名。

Mark Gatiss　マーク・ゲイティス（1966～）。イギリスの俳優・脚本家。『シャーロック』では脚本・制作に関わる一方で、シャーロック・ホームズの兄マイクロフト・ホームズ役で出演。

Chapter 12

White Teeth　小説『ホワイト・ティース』（2000）。北ロンドンに暮らす3つの家族（イギリス白人とジャマイカ系移民、バングラデシュ系移民、イギリスに定着した東欧系移民）を中心に物語が展開する。現代から時空を超えてセポイの反乱やジャマイカ大地震や第二次世界大戦へと場面を移す壮大な小説でありながら、1980年代から90年代までの風俗描写にも長けベストセラーとなった。チャンネル4がテレビドラマ化している（2002）。

Zadie Smith　ゼイディー・スミス（1975～）。イギリスの作家。『ホワイト・ティース』の登場人物アイリー・ジョーンズと同様、父がイギリス白人、母がジャマイカ系移民。

Goodness Gracious Me　『グッドネス・グレイシャス・ミー』。インド系の人々が作ったコント形式のお笑い番組（BBC）。ラジオ番組（1996～98）としてスタートし、テレビ番組となる（1998～2001）。

Meera Syal　ミーラ・サイヤル（1961～）。イギリスの作家、女優。インド系。

Anita and Me　小説『アニータと私』（1996）およびその映画化（2002）。詳細は本文参照。映画版では『グッドネス・グレイシャス・ミー』のメンバーの他、後に『ハリー・ポッター』シリーズでアーサー・ウィーズリーを演じるマーク・ウィリアムズが出演している。本邦未公開。

Britz　TVドラマ『ブリッツ』（2007）。詳細は本文参照。

East Is East　映画『ぼくの国、パパの国』（1999）。1970年代イングランド北部を舞台に、パキスタン系移民の父と白人の母の間に産まれた子供たちとの価値観の違いが織りなすコメディ。

Bend It Like Beckham　Chapter 5の注釈を参照。

Ae Fond Kiss　映画『やさしくキスをして』（2004）。スコットランドのグラスゴーを舞台にしたパキスタン系イスラム教徒のDJと敬虔なカトリック教徒の教師の恋の物語。

Kidulthood　映画『キダルトフッド』（2006）。暴力やドラッグに明け暮れるアフリカ・カリブ系のティーネイジャーの希望の見えない生活を描く。ロンドン中心部西側が舞台。本邦未公開。

Brick Lane　映画『ブリック・レーン』（2007）。親の取り決めでバングラデシュ系移民の男性と結婚した女性が、自分の生き方を見つけていくという物語。ロンドン中心部東側のバングラデシュ系住民が多く住む地区が舞台だが、当該地域の住民が「バングラデシュ系移民をステレオタイプ化している」としてボイコット運動を起こしたことでも知られる。原作は小説（2003）。

Small Island　TVドラマ『小さな島』（2009）。第二次世界大戦後の混乱期に「小さな島」すなわちジャマイカを出てイギリスで暮らす決意をした人々を描く群像劇。本邦未公開。主演：ナオミ・ハリス。原作は小説（2004）。

Chapter 13

Edward Snowden　エドワード・スノーデン（1983～）。アメリカの中央情報局（CIA）および国家安全保障局（NSA）の職員として勤務して、アメリカ合衆国の諜報活動に関わった後、その個人情報収集の実態を暴露し、逮捕命令が出されたことで有名になった。

Peeping Tom　映画『血を吸うカメラ』（1960）。覗くことによってしか性的欲求を満たせなくなったカメラマンの視点で描かれた作品で、当時は問題作として物議を醸した。監督：マイケル・パウエル、主演：モイラ・シアラー。なお、"Peeping Tom"とは、イギリスのゴダイヴァ夫人（Lady Godiva）の伝説に由来する。

Michael Powell　マイケル・パウエル（1905～90）。プロデューサーのエメリック・プレスバーガー（Emeric Pressburger, 1902～88）とともに、幻想的な独自の美学を確立したイギリスの映画監督。代表作に『黒水仙』（Black Narcissus, 1947）、『赤い靴』（The Red Shoes, 1948）、『ホフマン物語』（The Tales of Hoffmann, 1951）など。

Big Brother　TV番組『ビッグ・ブラザー』（1999～）。オランダで放送された「リアリティーTV」のタイプの番組で、カメラとマイクのセットされた家で人々が生活する様子を放送する。このフォーマットが各国に売られ、イギリスでも人気を博している。

George Orwell　ジョージ・オーウェル（1903～50）。イギリスの小説家、評論家。『動物農場』（Animal Farm, 1945）や『1984年』（Nineteen Eighty-Four, 1949）といった小説の他に、『ウィガン波止場への道』（The Road to Wigan Pier, 1937）や『カタロニア賛歌』（Homage to Catalonia, 1938）といった評論も有名。

Red Road　映画『レッド・ロード』（2006）。グラスゴーのCCTVオペレーターとして働く女性を主人公にした作品。監督：アンドレア・アーノルド。2014年時点で本邦未公開。

Closed Circuit　映画『クローズド・サーキット』（2013）。ロンドンを舞台にしたミステリ映画（詳細は本文参照）。監督：ジョン・クロウリー。2014年時点で本邦未公開。

Chapter 14

Children of Men　映画『トゥモロー・ワールド』（2006）。子供が生まれなくなり、人々は希望を失い社会が崩壊した近未来を

舞台にしたSF映画。原作はP. D. ジェイムズ（P. D. James, 1920〜）の同名の小説（1992、『人類の子供たち』として邦訳されている）。

Eastern Promises　映画『イースタン・プロミス』（2007）。ロンドンにおけるロシア・マフィアによる人身売買を主題としている。監督：デイヴィッド・クローネンバーグ、主演：ヴィゴ・モーテンセン、ナオミ・ワッツ。

It's a Free World　Chapter 4の注釈を参照。

Chapter 15

In the Name of the Father　映画『父の祈りを』（1993）。テロ事件容疑で逮捕されたアイルランド人が冤罪を明らかにすべく戦う。主演：ダニエル・デイ・ルイス、エマ・トンプソン、ピート・ポスルスウェイト。

Michael Collins　映画『マイケル・コリンズ』（1996）。アイルランド独立の立役者マイケル・コリンズの半生を描いた伝記映画。監督：ニール・ジョーダン、主演：リーアム・ニーソン。

The Wind That Shakes the Barley　映画『麦の穂をゆらす風』（2006）。アイルランド独立戦争前後のイギリスによる圧政やアイルランドの内部分裂が引き起こした悲劇などを描いた作品。監督：ケン・ローチ、主演：キリアン・マーフィー。

Neil Jordan　ニール・ジョーダン（1950〜）。アイルランドの映画監督。代表作に『クライング・ゲーム』（1992）、『マイケル・コリンズ』（1996）、『プルートで朝食を』（2005）など。

The Crying Game　映画『クライング・ゲーム』（1992）。IRAによる独立運動・テロ活動を背景にしたスリラー映画（詳細は本文参照）。監督：ニール・ジョーダン、主演：スティーヴン・レイ、ミランダ・リチャードソン。

JPCA 本書は日本出版著作権協会（JPCA）が委託管理する著作物です。
日本出版著作権協会 複写（コピー）・複製、その他著作物の利用については、事前にJPCA（電話03-3812-9424、e-mail:info@e-jpca.com）の許諾を得て下さい。なお、無断でコピー・スキャン・デジタル化等の複製をすることは著作権法上の例外を除き、著作権法違反となります。
http://www.jpca.jp.net/

▼スティール・写真提供

■表紙：（中央下）CAMERA PRESS/アフロ／（右下）REX FEATURES/アフロ
■ 1、3 頁：Everett Collection/アフロ 7、8 頁：Album/アフロ■ 15 頁：Jason Bell/Camera Press/アフロ■ 19 頁：Everett Collection/アフロ■ 21 頁：Visual Press Agency/アフロ■ 25 頁：アフロ■ 26 頁：Manchester City FC via AP/アフロ■ 31 頁：Album/アフロ■ 32 頁：REX FEATURES/アフロ■ 37 頁：Press Association/アフロ■ 38 頁：Photoshot/アフロ■ 43 頁：Visual Press Agency/アフロ■ 45 頁：Everett Collection/アフロ■ 51 頁：REX FEATURES/アフロ■ 55、56 頁：Album/アフロ■ 61 頁：Collection Christophel/アフロ■ 63 頁：Everett Collection/アフロ■ 67、68 頁：板倉厳一郎■ 73 頁：（右）板倉厳一郎／（左）Visual Press Agency/アフロ■ 79 頁：Everett Collection/アフロ■ 81 頁：Splash/AFLO■ 85 頁：Everett Collection/アフロ■ 86 頁：Album/アフロ

Reading Contemporary Britain:
15 Critical Views of Culture and Society
問題意識を持って読むイギリス 15 のトピック

2015 年 4 月 1 日　初版第 1 刷発行
2019 年 4 月 1 日　初版第 3 刷発行

著　者　Christopher J. Armstrong ／ Anthony Piccolo ／板倉厳一郎

発行者　森　信久
発行所　株式会社　松 柏 社
　　　　〒102-0072　東京都千代田区飯田橋1-6-1
　　　　TEL　03 (3230) 4813（代表）
　　　　FAX　03 (3230) 4857
　　　　http://www.shohakusha.com
　　　　e-mail: info@shohakusha.com

装　幀　小島トシノブ（NONdesign）
本文組版レイアウト　株式会社インターブックス
印　刷　シナノ書籍印刷株式会社
ISBN978-4-88198-704-9
略号＝ 704

Copyright © 2015 by Christopher J. Armstrong, Anthony Piccolo, Gen'ichiro Itakura

本書を無断で複写・複製することを禁じます。
落丁・乱丁は送料小社負担にてお取り替え致します。